ZONE OFFENSES
FOR MEN'S AND WOMEN'S BASKETBALL

Harry L. "Mike" Harkins
Jerry Krause

COACHES CHOICE

ISBN: 1-57167-139-0
Libreary of Congress Catalog Card Number: 97-67166

3 6626 10143 998 2

Book Layout: Michelle A. Summers
Cover Design: Deborah M. Bellaire
Cover Photos: Left—Courtesy of University of Michigan
              Right—Courtesy of University of Tennessee
Diagrams: James Hunt

Coaches Choice Books is an imprint of: Sagamore Publishing, Inc.
                                          P.O. Box 647
                                          Champaign, IL 61824-0647
                                          (800) 327-5557
                                          (217) 359-5940
                                          Fax: (217) 359-5975
                                          Web Site: http//www.sagamorepub.com

DEDICATION

This book is dedicated to my wife, Grace, who, along with being the love of my life, has been a working partner in the books I have written. Without her meticulous efforts on the diagrams and hours spent typing, they might never have been completed.

—H. L. H.

This book is dedicated to all those who have been given unique talents to play the great game of basketball. May they acknowledge that gift by always giving something back to the game. May this basketball coaching series be a gift to basketball from the authors who have received so much from the sport.

—J. K

ACKNOWLEDGMENTS

Grateful appreciation is expressed to the sources of my basketball knowledge, including: Russ Estey and Mike Krino, my high school coaches; Russ Beichly and Red Cochrane, my college coaches; Buck Hyser, who gave me my first coaching job; and the players who have played on my teams.

A final note of thanks goes to my children—Mike and his wife, Diane; Patti and her husband, Ric; and Jim and his wife, Jeanne—and my number one fans, my grandchildren, Shellee, Jamee, Mike, Shawn, and Walker.

A special acknowledgment goes to Jerry Krause for his diligent efforts in helping me complete this book.

CONTENTS

Chapter

PREFACE

These basketball coaching books for men and women coaches are a complete, comprehensive series of books designed to cover all prominent offensive and defensive techniques and strategies used in basketball, i.e., the X's and O's of the sport.

All coaches are reminded that all individual and team basketball is dependent upon individual fundamental skills. You need to ensure that your players are fundamentally sound in order to be able to execute offense and defense. Thus, fundamentals are always needed before the X's and O's of basketball.

Coaches at all levels will be able to utilize this complete series of men and women's books either as a complete package or as an integrated supplement to presently used offenses and defenses. There is something for every coach, from the novice to the most experienced basketball wizard. It is our intent to meet the needs of all coaches at all levels of play— develop and enjoy your special approach to the X's and O's of basketball.

How Zone Offenses Will Help You

In the not-too-distant past, player-to-player was the prevailing defense and playing against a zone was a novelty. The combination of factors that has changed this would include: the development of great one-on-one skills by offensive players, rules and interpretations that favor the offense, the presence of motion offenses that negate pressure-and-help player-to-player defensive rules, the refinement of zone defensive techniques, the use of the shot clock, and the use of zones on television by leading college teams. I would estimate that over half of all high school teams now use zones as their primary defense. On the college level, their popularity is on the rise and most teams use them to supplement their player-to-player defense. Because of this trend, it is necessary to have a comprehensive zone offensive attack and to include it in your weekly practice plan.

On a chapter-by-chapter basis, the winning zone offensive ideas are presented in the following manner.

Chapter One deals with "The Fundamentals of Zone Offense." These ideas will help you to develop a philosophy of zone offense which will, in turn, allow you to search for specific techniques as you examine the zone offensive ideas that follow.

Chapter Two covers "The Double Pinch Zone Offenses." This is a plan that offers opportunities for spontaneous play, and provides for offensive rebounding and frequent screens with two low-post players.

Chapter Three is "The Crossing Post Zone Offense." This plan involves enough motion to allow it to be used as an all-purpose offense and take care of offensive rebounding by keeping the two post players close to the basket.

Chapter Four explains "The Guard Loop Zone Offense." This plan tests the zone's corner and middle, provides many offside screens, and has an offensive perimeter that is constantly changing. The changing perimeter tends to confuse adjusting zones.

Chapter Five is "An Inside-Oriented Zone Offense" that seeks to get the ball inside the zone defense. Most of the shot options are accompanied by an offensive rebounding triangle. This makes the plan a very high-percentage offense. It may be run from a 1-2-2, 2-3, or 1-3-1 set, but two strong inside players are necessary for it to function at its best.

Chapter Six deals with "Player Movement Versus Zones." It contrasts moving and minimum-motion zone offenses by presenting the strengths and weaknesses of each. Specific offenses are featured that are examples of motion or relatively static plans.

Chapter Seven provides tips on "Practicing Winning Zone Offense." It includes motivational tips, practices management ideas, methods to improve your preseason and in-season zone offensive practices, and a zone scouting report.

The time is approaching when zone will become basketball's predominant defense. Today's coach must have a wide variety of zone offensive techniques. This book provides you with an abundance of game- and time-tested ideas.

—Mike Harkins and Jerry Krause

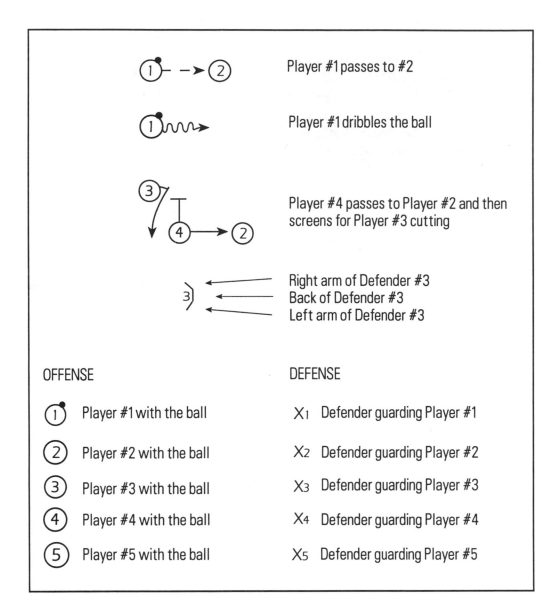

Player #1 passes to #2

Player #1 dribbles the ball

Player #4 passes to Player #2 and then screens for Player #3 cutting

Right arm of Defender #3
Back of Defender #3
Left arm of Defender #3

OFFENSE

1   Player #1 with the ball

2   Player #2 with the ball

3   Player #3 with the ball

4   Player #4 with the ball

5   Player #5 with the ball

DEFENSE

X_1 Defender guarding Player #1

X_2 Defender guarding Player #2

X_3 Defender guarding Player #3

X_4 Defender guarding Player #4

X_5 Defender guarding Player #5

CHAPTER 1

The Fundamentals of Zone Offense

Before designing a specific zone offense, you should consider the fundamentals of zone offense. They will provide a frame of reference that will allow you to make valid plans in terms of the players you have available, and types of zones you will face. Following are 20 zone offensive fundamentals.

1. Fast Break a Zone Defense

Zone defenses are vulnerable to fast-break attacks. The large defenders who play the inside positions of the zone probably play close to the basket on offense. This means the largest, and often the slowest, least agile defenders, must run the greatest distance to arrive at their vital areas of coverage. This creates three possibilities for the fast-breaking team. One is the initial/primary phase when you simply beat them downcourt; two is the trailer or secondary phase when perimeter trailer shots may be available; and three is the defensive invert stage when the small defenders, who probably were the first players back on defense, must move out to cover the perimeter, and only the big players cover the inside. This is the time when trailer lay-ups or early offense (including the three-point field goal) may provide easy baskets.

2. Split Zone Defense

One of the first rules most coaches learn about zone offense is the rule of opposites. This is also called putting offensive perimeter players in the "gaps" of the zone.

When the defense has an even front, you should use an odd-front offense. When the defense has an odd front, you should have an even front. Diagram 1-1 shows the defense in a 2-3 zone, and the offense in a 1-3-1 formation. This 1-3-1 alignment "splits" the 2-3 zone and gives the advantage to the offense by blurring the defenders' areas of coverage.

If the offense chooses to use a 2-3 alignment versus a 2-3 zone, the defense "matches" the offense. This gives the advantage to the defense because they can utilize their zone slides and still have the player-on-player advantages of a player-to-player defense. See Diagram 1-2.

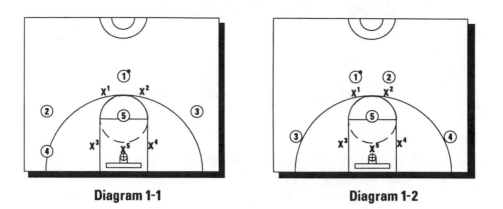

| Diagram 1-1 | Diagram 1-2 |

This same principle applies when playing against odd-front zones. Diagram 1-3 shows the offense splitting or playing in the gaps of a 1-3-1 zone with a 2-3 formation. Diagram 1-4 shows a 1-3-1 offense being matched by a 1-3-1 zone.

Therefore, the offense should seek to gain an advantage by using the rule of opposites in aligning your offense against the opposing zone defenses. Get in the gaps.

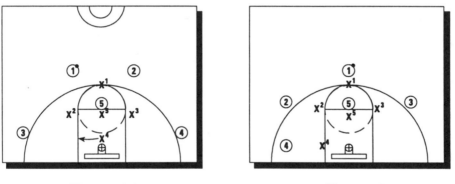

| Diagram 1-3 | Diagram 1-4 |

3. Expect to Shoot Outside

It is a simple fact that more outside shots are taken against zone defenses than against player-to-player defenses. One must anticipate this and devote ample practice time to zone spot-shooting. Against even-front zones, the most frequent perimeter shots by teams (using the rule of opposites) are shown in Diagram 1-5.

Against odd-front zones, the most frequent perimeter shots taken are shown in Diagram 1-6.

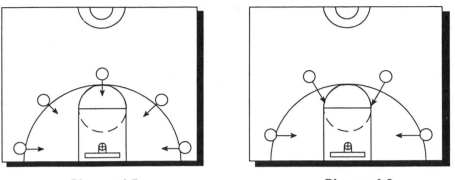

Diagram 1-5　　　　　　　　　　**Diagram 1-6**

A composite of the two would provide the areas from which players must practice to become adept at shooting from the perimeters of all zones. See Diagram 1-7. Shooting practice should proceed from the "inside out" in these perimeter circles, i.e., from about 15 to 21 foot distances.

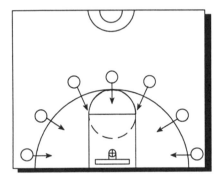

Diagram 1-7

These seven spots can be the basis of practice games played each day. For example, each perimeter player may be required to make a round of the zone perimeter shots in which he or she must make each shot in two attempts, or start over. The number "two" can be adjusted according to the skill level of your team. For example, secondary school players might use a goal of 1 in 3 at three-point field-goal distance and 1 in 2 attempts inside the arc.

4. Overload the Zone Defense

An overload is a situation where two to three perimeter players, plus a post player, are placed on one side of the court in order to thoroughly test the defenders on that side. Diagram 1-8 shows an overload situation against a 2-3 zone.

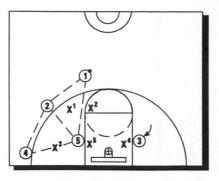

Diagram 1-8

Note that the overloading offensive players are arranged in passing triangles that facilitate moving the ball. Also, be aware that (3) is positioned to provide for offside offensive rebounding. Some teams use an overload and do not provide for offside rebounding. The net result of this practice is negating an important part of a complete offensive plan—offensive rebounding.

5. Overshift the Zone Defense

Every team should have a rule against zone defenses that no shot should be taken on the perimeter until the ball goes second side. Otherwise, the defense has a definite rebounding edge. Diagram 1-9 shows a team taking an outside shot on the initial penetration pass. The result is that the defenders are stationed in a rebound triangle, and inside the offensive players. One way to teach this is to tell your players to spread the defense early by moving the ball to establish ballside, then swing the ball to the second side. After that, look for the best shot and penetrate and pitch and move for a shot.

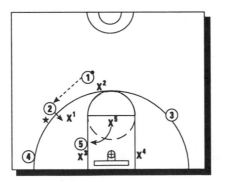

Diagram 1-9

So it is wise to *at least* go second side, and even to penetrate the zone's perimeter with a pass or dribble before taking a perimeter shot. Another method of spreading the defenders and getting them out of their symmetrical alignment is the "skip" pass to the second side. A skip pass is a pass that bypasses one of the offensive players. Diagram 1-10 shows wing player (2) throwing a "skip" pass to wing player (3) that bypasses point player (1).

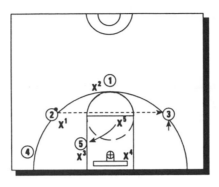

Diagram 1-10

6. Vary the Offensive Perimeter

The modern zone defense is in a stage of development where most teams using it attempt to make adjustments that permit them to "match" the offensive perimeter. Having a static offensive perimeter makes the job too easy for the defense. It is wise to change the front of the offense from even to odd to even, etc., to prevent the defense from gaining an advantage by "matching" the offense. This can be done by moving the ball *and* players against the zone.

7. Have a Rebound Plan

Most zone defenses desire to limit the offense to one hurried outside shot. Because of this fact, the zone offensive players must move the ball and be strategically aligned. Ideally, this strategic alignment includes a rebound triangle. It also involves teaching the offensive players that they must not stand still as the ball is passed around the perimeter. Rather they must be in position to receive the ball is an open passing lane 15-18 feet from the ball when it is on their side of the court and in position to rebound when they are on the offside. For example, in Diagram 1-11, wing player (2) plays free throw line-high when the ball is on his or her side. This creates the proper passing angle and distance to assure that the pass will be completed.

However, when the ball is taken to the other side of the court, (2) must think about rebounding and assume a lower position. Also, note that (3) moved up to receive (1)'s pass. When players stand still, they not only lose rebounding position, but the defenders can anticipate where they are and have a better chance for an interception. See Diagram 1-12.

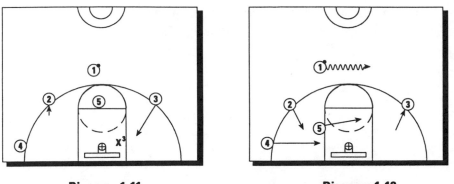

Diagram 1-11   **Diagram 1-12**

Finally, players must be taught to charge the boards against zones. It must be pointed out to them that it is very difficult for zone teams to devise block-out rules and, therefore, second shots are easier to acquire. For example, in Diagram 1-11, when (1) or (2) shoots it is possible for (3) to rebound the offside effectively by blocking *in* or pinning X3 inside the lane and obtaining the offside rebound (where 80% of missed shots will come).

8. Test the Zone's Corner

When the ball is passed from the front to the side and then to the corner against a zone, the defense must execute one of two maneuvers. Either their big player must cover the corner or they must execute a corner adjustment of some sort. Having their big player cover the corner lowers their rebounding chances, and the corner adjustments to keep the big man inside can lead to costly defensive errors. An example of a corner adjustment would be the "bump and run" maneuver made famous by Jud Heathcote's Michigan State teams. This 2-3 zone covers the front-to-wing pass initially with the ballside wing defender (X3 in Diagram 1-13). Defender X3 comes out, puts his or her hands up, and drops off as soon as the front defender on that side (X1) can get to the ball.

When the ball is then passed to the corner, X3 covers the corner. See Diagram 1-14. This "bump and run" maneuver is very difficult for X3 to execute, but it permits X5 to stay inside to form a rebound triangle with X2 and X4.

This defensive corner maneuver is a form of robbing Peter to pay Paul (as is most corner coverage), but you must test the corner or short corner (Diagram 1-13) to force the adjustment.

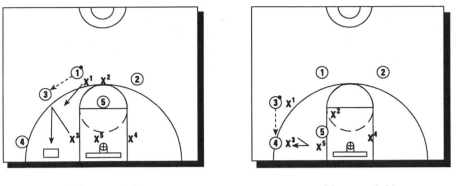

Diagram 1-13   Diagram 1-14

9. Test the Zone's Middle

If you place a tall, good shooter at the high post (above the free throw line) position, the zone will usually cover the player in one of two ways. They will have the offside guard of a 2-3 zone jam the high-post area. See X2 in Diagram 1-15.

Or they will bring an inside player up to cover (5). See X5 of the 2-3 zone in Diagram 1-16.

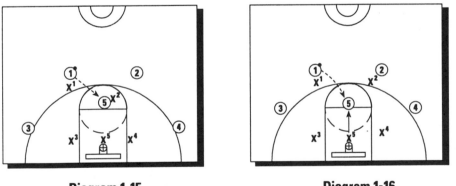

Diagram 1-15   Diagram 1-16

When they cover (5) with an offside defender, it opens up the perimeter and when they bring a big player up, it makes them vulnerable inside.

10. Make Post-to-Post Passes

The two basic post-to-post passes are high-post-to-low-post and low-post-to-the-high-post breaking down.

High-to-Low-Post Pass

When the ball is passed to the high post receiver, (4) in Diagram 1-17, turns to face the basket, very often the middle defender X5 will come up to cover (4). When this occurs, an offensive player under the basket in a lay-up slot, (5), may be wide open.

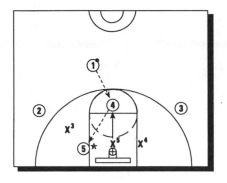

Diagram 1-17

Low-to-High-Post Pass

Another strong maneuver is for the ballside wing player, (2) in Diagram 1-18, to pass to the low-post player (5) as he or she moves one-third of the way to the ballside corner to the short corner. High-post player (4) then breaks down into the hole created by X5's move toward (5).

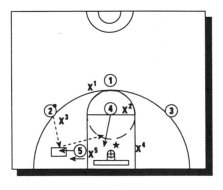

Diagram 1-18

(4) and (5) should consider themselves as inside partners who always look to pass to each other, i.e., when one player gets the ball the other inside player always looks to get open to receive a pass and test/compress the inside of the zone defense with a post-to-post pass.

11. Screen the Zone

There are many ways to screen a zone defense. Two examples are the double stack and the offside screen.

The Double Stack

When teams run a stack play against a zone (see Diagram 1-19), they, in effect, attempt to trap or screen the zone players inside on both sides of the zone and prevent them from moving out to cover their side.

This maneuver will often result in a jump shot on one of the sides. It may also lead to a situation that spreads the zone defenders to a degree that a pass can be made from the point to a player inside the zone for a power lay-up shot. See Diagram 1-20.

The rule for any player screening the zone is to screen, step up to the ball as the cutter uses the screen and post up when the cutter gets the ball (Diagram 1-20).

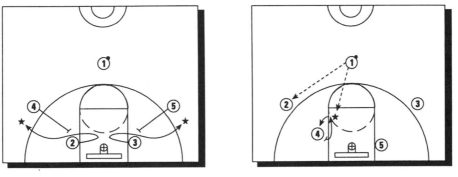

Diagram 1-19   Diagram 1-20

The Offside Screen

The offside screen is accomplished by passing the ball to one side of the zone and shifting the defense in that direction. Diagram 1-21 shows (1) pass to (3) and cut to the offside.

The ball is then reversed to the other side as the screener (4) disallows the zone from covering (1). See Diagram 1-22. Note that (4) will use the screen-step to ball-post up technique when screening the zone.

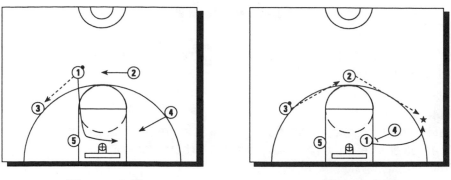

Diagram 1-21   **Diagram 1-22**

12. Place your Personnel in the Proper Areas

In the player-to-player game, the defensive team determines the defensive match-ups. This is not true in the zone game. The defense sets itself, and you may place your offensive players where you wish. Why not: (A) put your big post player against their small inside player, (B) place your good shooter or driver against their weak defender, or (C) put your strong rebounder on the side of their weak rebounder and then plan your shots to gain a rebounding advantage? This point is that it is possible to place your offensive zone players in positions that give you an advantage in terms of personnel match-ups.

13. Run your Player-to-Player Offense as a Secondary Zone Attack

There are some games against zone defenses when your team's zone attack is completely ineffective. The opposition may have done an excellent job scouting; their particular zone slides may work well against your zone maneuvers; or maybe the personnel match-ups are in their favor. Whatever the cause, it is wise to resort to your player-to-player offense as a secondary attack. This should be attempted only after a thorough examination of your player-to-player offense's zone potential. Most offenses have some elements that are adaptable. This may include such player-to-player components as reversing the ball, stick plays, offside screens, or dribble entries. Once this determination has been made, those player offenses that apply should be run in practice against zone defenses. This will ensure their validity and condition the players to the possible shot options. Then, on game nights when your zone offense is having problems, you can call time out, switch to your player attack, and give the opposition a new set of problems. Even if this ploy does not result in easy baskets, it may take the zone out of its rhythm, or distort their knowledge of your zone plan. Then when you return to your standard zone offense, their zone may not be confident or effective.

The practice of using your player offense against zones is also functional against changing, disguised, or combination defenses. When in doubt, run your player offense.

14. Read the Zone's Intent

Early in the ball game, you must try to determine what the zone is attempting to accomplish. Are they causing pressure on the perimeter either by double-teaming, or attempting to steal the ball? If so, this is the time to get the ball inside. Are they just content to jam the lane and give you the outside shot? If so, this may be the time to insert a pure shooter who lacks other skills, or to hold the ball (when the rules permit) until they come out to cover the perimeter. Scouting is especially important in this regard because you can develop maneuvers to counter their plan. This might include a special play, a stall game, a change in personnel, but at a minimum, it provides an opportunity to inform your players about the nature of their zone.

15. Hold the Ball

Every team should have a zone stall. You may be ahead of a superior team that because of their personnel (big and slow), plays nothing but zone defense. Forcing them to come out and change from their zone defense could make the situation difficult for them. If your game has a shot clock, you will still need this option for a few possessions.

16. Have a Pressure Defense Ready

There are games against zones when they completely control the game's tempo, usually slowing the game. When this occurs, you should have a pressure defense available to control game tempo. It is also wise at this time to stress your fast-break game.

17. Freeze Their Defensive Perimeters

Many zone defenses have the ability to match the initial offensive perimeter. Once this has been accomplished, it is difficult for them to adjust to the problems that cutters present. Therefore, it is wise for the offense to first pass the ball around the entire perimeter. This may freeze their defense in a particular shape and a subsequent cutter could destroy their player relationship. Therefore, the rule is to "perimeter pass early" in a given possession.

18. Test Their Second Side

Another reason for moving the ball against zones is the fact that many zone's defensive teams cheat to the first side. Diagram 1-23 shows X1 is at the point and X2 is on the free throw line. Player X2's rule is to cover the first pass to a wing. This matches the first side and keeps big defender X5 inside when the ball goes to the corner. See Diagram 1-24.

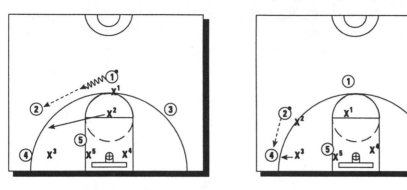

Diagram 1-23   **Diagram 1-24**

However, if the offense will move the ball to the offside (second side), the defense must send a big player (X4 in Diagram 1-25) up to cover (3). See Diagram 1-26.

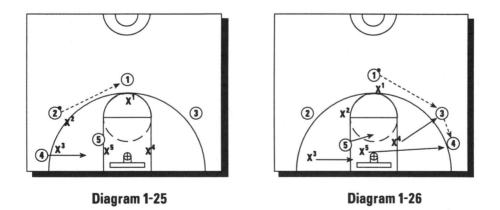

Diagram 1-25   **Diagram 1-26**

This perimeter pass to test their second side may also force big defender X5 to cover the wing and corner if (3) chooses to pass to (4). The practice of shooting after the initial penetration pass often provides the defense an easy defensive match-up and a rebounding advantage.

19. Move the Ball at an Arrhythmic Tempo—Use Shot and Pass Fakes

Most zone defensive teams practice their zone slides by having the offense pass from one player to the next in a rhythmic fashion. Because of this, it is wise to have your team move the ball at an arrhythmic tempo that includes such individual moves as rotation and penetration dribbles, skip passes, and turnbacks. This forces the defense to make adjustments in their slides that they may not have practiced. This, in turn, may lead in defensive errors, and easy baskets for your team.

Dribbling with a purpose; use rotation dribbles to stretch coverage (dribble chase and loop as seen in Diagram 1-27) forces defenders X1 and X2 to decide on coverage and cutter responsibility. Penetration dribbles are used primarily just after a pass is received and before the shifting zone is set or again matches the offensive alignment. This often occurs on the "second side" pass. Another critical technique to master against the zone defense, which is ball oriented, is to show the ball (overhead pass position) and use pass fakes to move/freeze the zone and shot fakes from triple-threat position to freeze defenders and force them to cover the ballhandler.

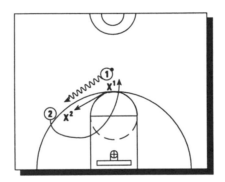

Diagram 1-27

20. Overcome the Fear of Zones

My teams (Harkins) played nothing but zone defenses for ten consecutive seasons. We became known as a "zone team" and many teams altered their practice week to meet this "different" team. Zone defenses are much more common today, but I feel that coaches still create a fear of zone teams by their mystical approach to them. This gives the opposition a psychological edge. Working against zone defenses should be a standard component of each week's practice plan. Practices during the week in which you play the zone team should be altered only slightly in terms of the specific information provided by the scouting report. Build your team's confidence in attacking zone defenses.

These fundamentals of zone offense offer many ways to attack zone defenses. Choose the ideas that best fit your situation and use them as a shopping list as you study the specific zone offenses in the next six chapters.

21. Catch the Ball with Jump Stops

On the perimeter, it is important to force the zone defense to react quickly and cover every pass. This can be done by catching every pass in a basketball-ready position; with a jump stop, ball in triple threat, ready to pass-dribble-shoot. The ball may then be taken overhead to show the ball for shot or pass fakes. When this is done quickly with proper spacing (most potential pass receivers within 15-18 feet of the ball—and open) it puts tremendous pressure on the zone defense.

Legendary Hall of Fame coach Ralph Miller (Oregon State, Iowa, Wichita State) states that the jump stop and quick, accurate air passes are the most important weapons against the zone.

The Double Pinch Zone Offense

The Double Pinch Zone Offense presents many problems to the zone defenders. It sends cutters through the zone that may lead to either overshift or overload formations, and rebounding potential is maintained throughout the plays by the presence of the two big players in the double-post positions. The offense is also easily converted from its basic 1-2-2 "jug" set to a 2-3 "elbow" formation. This versatility of shape permits the offensive players to split even- or odd-front zones.

Personnel Alignment for the 1-2-2 Jug Formation

When utilizing the 1-2-2 jug formation, the point position is occupied by the team's best ballhandler and team leader, (1). Player (1) must initiate each new play sequence. Wing players (2) and (3) also must be adequate ballhandlers, and strong outside shooters. The post players (4) and (5) are the two key rebounders, who must be able to score with their backs to the basket. See Diagram 2-1.

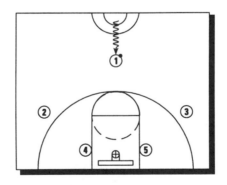

Diagram 2-1

The Basic Plays

Guard-Through Play

Point guard (1) passes to either wing (as to (2) in Diagram 2-2) and cuts down the middle. The point guard is replaced at the point by the offside wing player, (3). Player (1) may then cut to the offside wing or the ballside corner. When (1) cuts to the offside wing area, the ball is quickly reversed by way of (3). This attempt to catch the defense overshifted is aided by (5), who screens the nearest zone defenders and impedes their path to (1). See Diagrams 2-2 and 2-3.

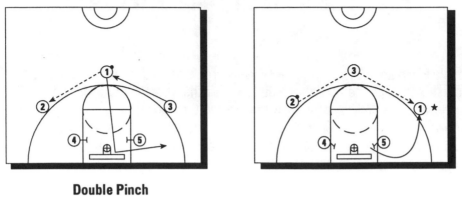

**Double Pinch
Diagram 2-2**

Diagram 2-3

When (1) makes the cut down the lane and to the ballside corner, an overload formation is created with (2) at the wing, (1) in the corner, (3) at the point, and (4) in the ballside post position. Note that (1)'s cut to the corner was facilitated by post player (4)'s screening the nearest zone defender. It is from this pinching action of (4) and (5) that the offense derives its name. See Diagram 2-4. Their technique is screen in, step to the ball, and post up on the pass to the cutter. The cutter may use the screen for a closer two-point shot or a three-point field-goal attempt.

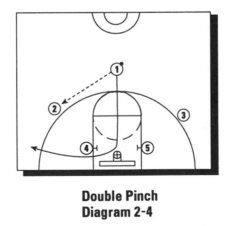

**Double Pinch
Diagram 2-4**

The overload is then utilized until wing player (2) decides to change it. Wing (2) may do this in either of two ways. Player (2) may pass to (3) and screen down for (1). This keys (3) to dribble toward the offside, and cause the zone to shift in that direction. (See Diagram 2-6). Player (2) screens the nearest zone defender to (1); (1) moves up to the wing for a pass from (3) and a possible jump shot (see Diagram 2-6).

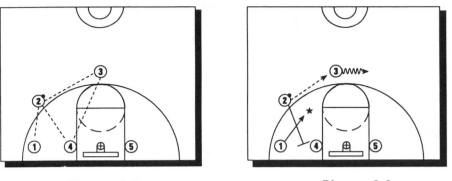

| Diagram 2-5 | Diagram 2-6 |

If (1) is not open, (2) continues across the lane using (5)'s screen to balance the formation or uses (4)'s screen on a "comeback" to the ballside (see Diagram 2-7).

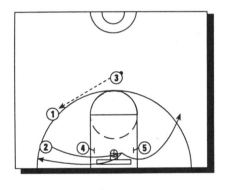

Diagram 2-7

Wing player (2) may also switch the overload with a dribble chase maneuver. (2) does this by dribbling to point player (3). This clears (3) down the lane and gives (3) the option of cutting to the offside wing area (see Diagram 2-8) or to (1)'s side to form an overload (see Diagram 2-9). In either case, (1) moves to the wing area and the post players screen the zone in their pinching action.

All throughout this motion, the middle player of the three perimeter players has the option of cutting through, or remaining in, the same position and moving the ball. This decision will determine the shape of the perimeter. The dribble chase technique may also result in a "loop" maneuver by (3) as seen in Diagram 2-9. In that event (1) would remain in the corner.

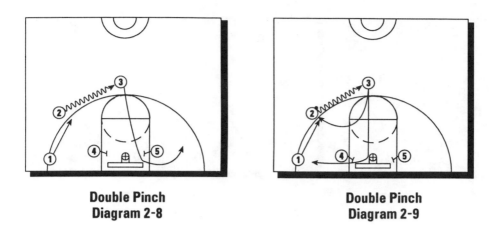

Double Pinch
Diagram 2-8

Double Pinch
Diagram 2-9

Outside-Cut Play

This time, point guard (1) passes to a wing player (as to (2) in Diagram 2-10) and makes an outside cut. Player (3) takes the point, as (2) returns the ball to (1), and cuts over the post player (4), and down the middle.

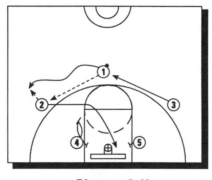

Diagram 2-10

Player (2) then has the option of cutting to the offside wing area to create an overshift maneuver (see Diagram 2-11) or cutting to the ballside corner to create an overload (see Diagram 2-12).

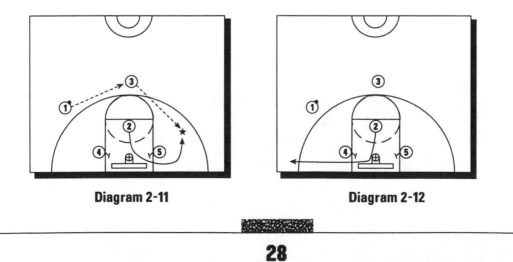

Diagram 2-11

Diagram 2-12

When (2)'s cut results in an overload, (1) becomes the middle player and may change the formation by passing to (3) and cutting through, or using a dribble chase on (3).

Note that inside players (4) and (5) will use the screen, step-up, post-up technique whenever their screen on the outside zone player is used.

Dribble-Entry Play

This time (1) chooses to initiate a play by dribbling at a wing player (as at (2) in Diagram 2-13). Player (2) may then cut to the ballside corner to form an overload or cut across the lane and to the offside wing to create an overshift situation. See Diagram 2-14. In either case, (3) replaces (1) at the point. (2) may also loop back to the dribbler (1)'s starting position. In that event, (3) holds position.

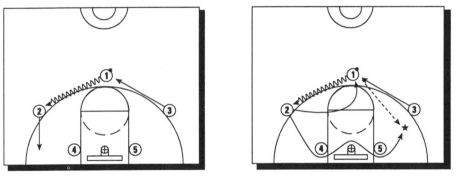

| Diagram 2-13 | Diagram 2-14 |

After passing to (3), (1) drops low. Many times the zone players will anticipate and fight hard to get over (5)'s screen. In this event, (1) may be wide open for a two-point shot or a trey if needed. This is a strong "last-second shot" maneuver against zones. See Diagram 2-15.

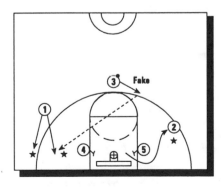

Diagram 2-15

Inside (Post) Motion

When (1) makes the initial pass to a wing and does not cut, it keys an inside rotation by post players (4) and (5). In Diagram 2-16, (1) does not cut after the initial pass to wing (2). This tells the offside post (5) to cut to the ballside high post area. If (2) can pass to (5), (5) may shoot or look for (4) inside the zone on a post-to-post pass. Note that (3) dropped down to assume an offside rebounding position.

Post Motion
Diagram 2-16

If (2) cannot get the ball to (5), (4) clears across the lane and (5) drops down to the low-post position above the block. If (5) is still not open, (2) reverses the ball to (3) by way of (1). See Diagram 2-17. The offense is then balanced. At this time, the point guard (1) may key a new play as shown in Diagram 2-18.

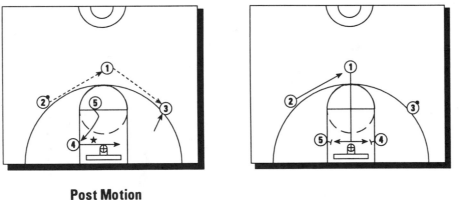

Post Motion
Diagram 2-17

Diagram 2-18

Scatter Option

The Scatter Option is a simple one, but very functional against matching, adjusting-type zones. Once (1) passes to a wing (as to (2) in Diagram 2-19), both (1) and the offside wing, (3), will be cutters. Some examples are shown in Diagrams 2-20 through 2-22.

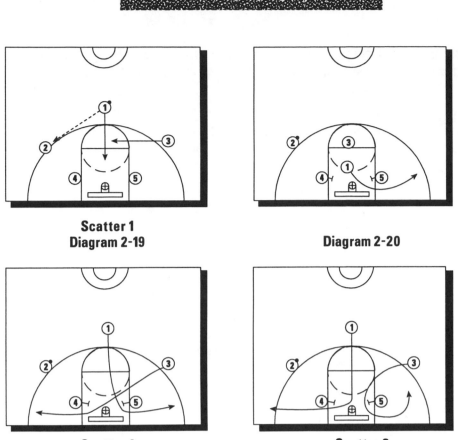

Scatter 1
Diagram 2-19

Diagram 2-20

Scatter 2
Diagram 2-21

Scatter 3
Diagram 2-22

Player (2) then does one of two things: pass to an open player and move to the point. See Diagram 2-23.

Or, if no one gained an advantage by all this cutting, (2) may dribble to the point. See Diagram 2-24.

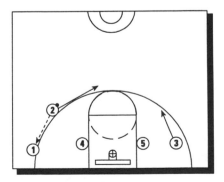

Diagram 2-23

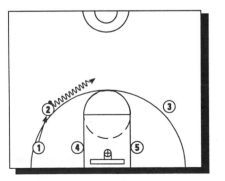

Diagram 2-24

Then the next pass from the point to a wing (as from (2) to (3) in Diagram 2-25) keys another scatter option with (2) and (1) acting as the cutters and (3) as the passer.

Again (4) and (5) may facilitate the cuts by screening the zone players (screen, step up, post up). This scatter option phase of the offense may be called by the coach during a time-out period, or by (1) with an oral and/or hand signal.

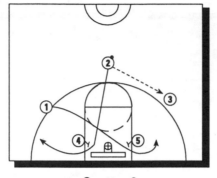

Scatter 2
Diagram 2-25

2-3 Elbow Formation

When the 2-3 elbow set is used as the primary offense, the middle player of the three perimeter players is still the player who keys the plays. However, the inside perimeter player, (3) in Diagram 2-26, is given the option of changing sides of the court. This move will switch the middle player assignment.

Once a middle player has been established, he or she may call:

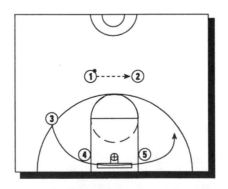

Diagram 2-26

Guard-Through Play from the 2-3 Set

In Diagram 2-27, middle player (2) keys the guard-through play by passing to wing (3) and cutting down the lane. Player (2) may then cut to (3)'s corner and form an overload (see Diagram 2-28) or to the offside wing for an overshift play (see Diagram 2-29).

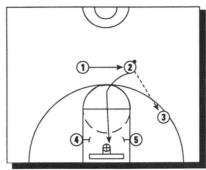

Guard Through
Diagram 2-27

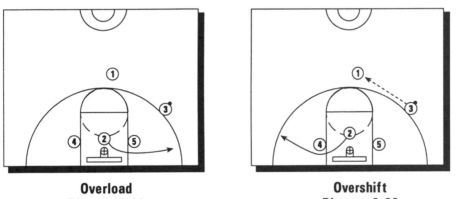

Overload
Diagram 2-28

Overshift
Diagram 2-29

Outside Cut from the 2-3 Set

To start an outside cut play from the 2-3 set, middle player (1) passes to (3) an makes an outside cut. Player (3) returns the ball to (1) and cuts down the lane to overload or overshift the zone. See Diagrams 2-30 and 2-31.

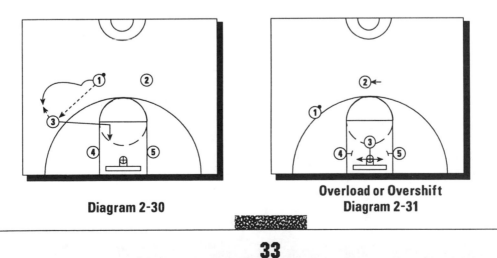

Diagram 2-30

Overload or Overshift
Diagram 2-31

Once these plays are over, (2) would key the return to the elbow set by dribbling away from (1) to move (1) out front. Diagram 2-32 shows this occurring after the overload play and Diagram 2-33 shows it after an overshift play.

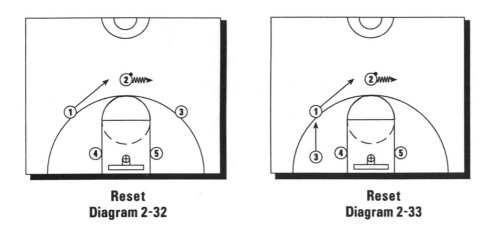

Reset
Diagram 2-32

Reset
Diagram 2-33

Dribble-Entry Play

In Diagram 2-34, (1) dribbles at and may clear (3) to the ballside corner to form an overload play or to the offside wing for an overshift play. See Diagram 2-35. This may also result in a "loop" option (Diagram 2-34).

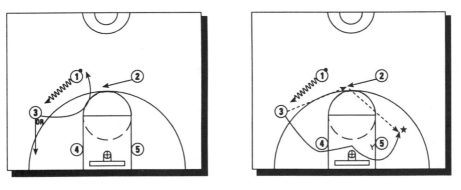

Diagram 2-34

Diagram 2-35

From there, (2) can return the offense to the elbow set by dribbling away from (1). See Diagram 2-36.

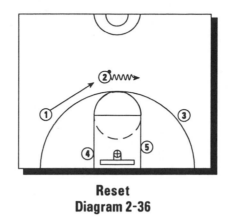

Reset
Diagram 2-36

Inside Rotation/Post Motion

The Inside Rotation may be run when the middle player (1) in Diagram 2-37 makes the initial pass to (3) and does not cut through.

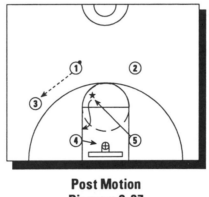

Post Motion
Diagram 2-37

Scatter Option

The Scatter Option from the 2-3 elbow set is again keyed by a hand or oral signal. Player (1) passes to (3) and both (1) and (2) cut through. See Diagram 2-38. Player (3) may hit the open player and return to the point (see Diagram 2-39) or not pass, and dribble to the point (see Diagram 2-40).

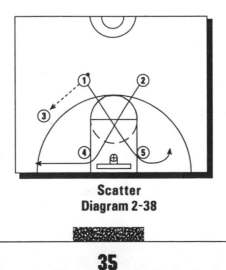

Scatter
Diagram 2-38

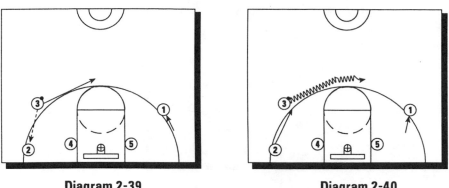

Diagram 2-39   **Diagram 2-40**

Auxiliary Plays

These auxiliary plays may be used to meet a special situation, take advantage of a particular skill of one of your players, or simply give the offense depth as the season progresses.

1-2-2 Jug Set

Crosscourt Lob Play
In Diagram 2-41 (1) passes to (3) and that shifts the zone in (3)'s direction. Player (2) then screens the nearest zone player to (1). Player (1) slides to the offside wing area and receives a crosscourt pass from (3) for a jump shot (usually a three-point attempt). Player (4) may aid this play by moving up to help (2) screen the zone. See Diagram 2-42.

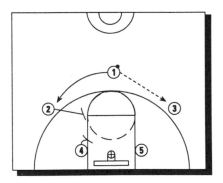

Second Side Lob
Diagram 2-41

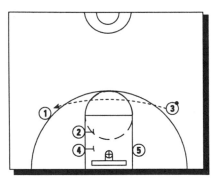

Diagram 2-42

If (1) cannot get a shot, (2) loops down and under (5) and (3) takes the point. Player (1) reverses the ball to (2) by way of (3). See Diagram 2-43. Player (3) may then cut through and initiate a new play.

In the event (3) cannot make the crosscourt pass to (1), (3) dribbles to the point and (2) still cuts to the offside wing area using (5)'s screen. See Diagram 2-44.

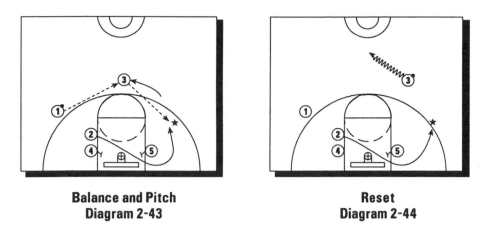

Balance and Pitch
Diagram 2-43

Reset
Diagram 2-44

Post-Out Sequence

When post players (4) and (5) are not dominant inside and are adequate shooters, the post-out sequence may be run. Player (1) calls this maneuver with a hand signal and a dribble to one side. This tells the offside post (5) to move out front and receive the ball from (1). See Diagram 2-45. This changes the basic formation from a one-player front to a two-player front.

This wide box formation with 15-18 foot spacing tends to spread the zone and may leave post (4) or wings (2) and (3) open. Player (5) may then return to ball to (1), or pass to (3) and cut through. Post (4) may also cut to the ball. (5) would go opposite (4) inside when that occurs. See Diagram 2-46.

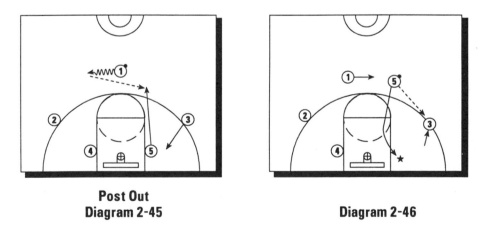

Post Out
Diagram 2-45

Diagram 2-46

Player (1) then moves back to the ballside. When (1) receives the ball, it keys the new offside post (4) to move out front. See Diagram 2-47.

From there, the same process may be repeated. See Diagrams 2-48 and 2-49.

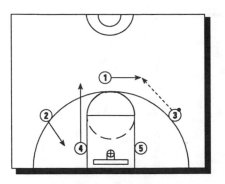

Diagram 2-47

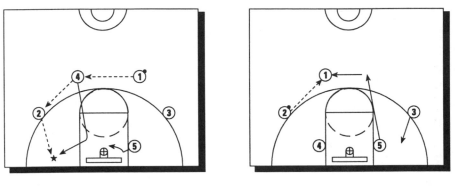

Diagram 2-48   **Diagram 2-49**

The spreading of the zone followed by the penetrating cut of the post will usually lead to an easy outside shot or a power-up play for the post. If (4) receives a pass from (2) in the short corner (Diagram 2-48), (5) may cut across the lane for a possible post-to-post pass.

2-3 Elbow Set

Pass-and-Screen-Away Play

The middle player of the elbow set, (1) in Diagram 2-50, passes to the player in the offside guard position, (2). This shifts the zone in (2)'s direction as (1) screens down for (3), who moves out front. This screen may pin down the zone defender, who would move up to cover (3). It helps if (2), upon receiving the pass from (1), takes a dribble toward the wing position on his or her side and then passes to (3) for the shot.

Player (1) may then loop to that side or cross over as shown in Diagram 2-51.

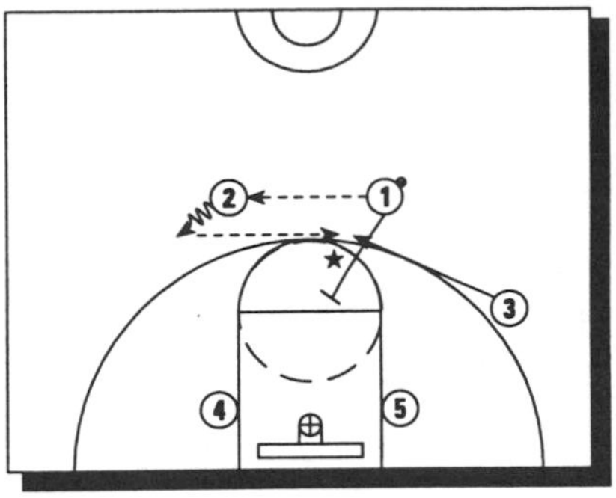

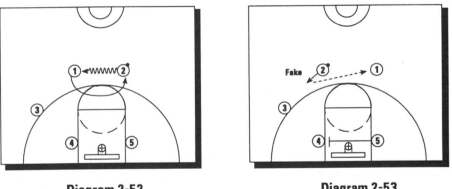

**Screen Down
Diagram 2-50**

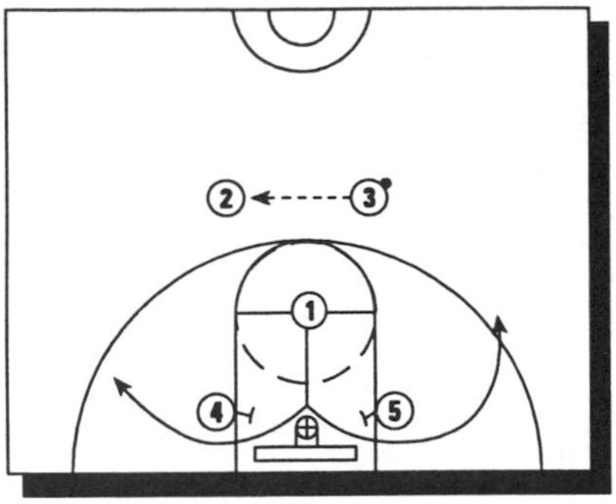

Diagram 2-51

2-3 Elbow-Lob Play

This is a super lob play that has a history of great success. The offside guard (2) keys the play by dribbling at the middle player of the elbow set (1). This loop clears (1) across the lane to replace (2). See Diagram 2-52.

Player (2) fakes to (3) to pull the wing defender up and then pivots and throws a crisp chest pass to (1). At the same time, (5) has moved across the lane and screened the defender on (4). See Diagram 2-53.

Diagram 2-52

Diagram 2-53

Player (4) moves across the lane and (5) continues his or her cut to screen for (3). See Diagram 2-54.

Player (1) looks first for (4) and then lobs crosscourt to (3) coming off (5)'s screen. See Diagram 2-55.

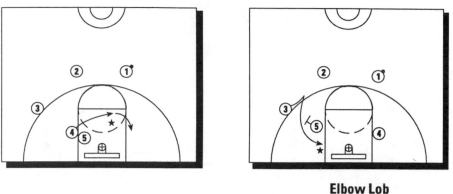

Diagram 2-54

Elbow Lob
Diagram 2-55

If (3) is not open, (1) holds up, and (3) crosses the lane using (4)'s screen to return the elbow set. See Diagram 2-56. (4) will screen in, step up to the ball (1), and post up when (3) receives the pass.

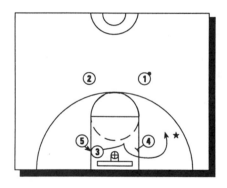

Diagram 2-56

Twice-Around Elbow-Lob Play

This play is keyed by the middle player of the elbow set, (1) in Diagram 2-57, who passes to the ballside wing (3) and cuts down and around the offside post (5). Player (3) then quickly reverses the ball to (1) by way of (2). After passing, (2) also cuts down and around the offside post (4). Player (3) replaces (2) at the point. See Diagram 2-58.

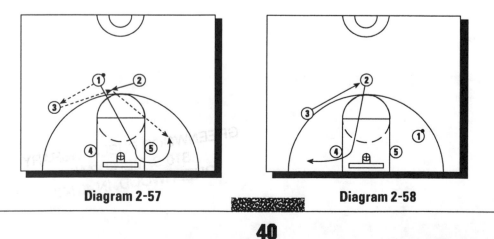

Diagram 2-57

Diagram 2-58

At this juncture, (5) moves half-way to the ballside corner (short corner) and assumes a triple-threat position. From here, one of two things may occur: (5) may be open for a shot (see Diagram 2-59) or (5) may be covered. If this is the case, (1) lobs crosscourt to (2) using (4)'s offside screen. See Diagram 2-60.

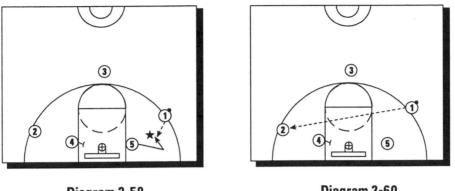

Diagram 2-59   **Diagram 2-60**

It is extremely difficult for the zone to cover both (5) and (2) on this play.

This Double-Post Pinch Offense may be used against even- or odd-front zones. It permits the perimeter players to play in a spontaneous fashion and keeps the two key rebounders close to the basket. It is an ideal plan for a team with three mobile outside players and two strong inside players.

CHAPTER 3

The Crossing Post Zone Offense

The Crossing Post Zone Offense probes zone defenses in many ways. The inside motion of the crossing post players constantly tests the middle of the defense, and the pass-and-move-away cuts of the perimeter players penetrate, screen, and present a changing picture to the outside zone defenders.

Personnel Alignment

The basic set consists of a high and low post on the same side of the lane (see (4) and (5) in Diagram 3-1) and three perimeter players who start in a balanced alignment with (1) at the point and (2) and (3) at their respective wing positions. Player (1) is the team's best ballhandler, who must be able to initiate the offense under pressure. Players (2) and (3) must also be mobile players and adequate outside shooters. Players (4) and (5) are strong rebounders who have the ability to score with their backs to the basket.

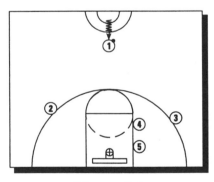

Diagram 3-1

The Basic Pattern

The basic pattern usually begins with (1) passing to the wing player away from the post players and cutting away from his or her pass. This tells posts (4) and (5) to cut in a crossing motion (X it) to the ballside. After passing, (1) may loop inside (4) and (5) as in Diagram 3-2, exchange with (3) as in Diagram 3-3, or receive a screen from (3) as (1) moves to the offside for a possible crosscourt lob pass from (2) outside the arc, as in Diagrams 3-4 and 3-5. In all three situations, (3) replaces (1) at the point.

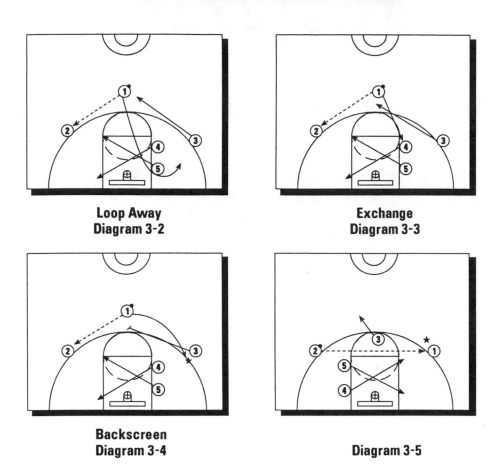

Loop Away
Diagram 3-2

Exchange
Diagram 3-3

Backscreen
Diagram 3-4

Diagram 3-5

As (4) and (5) cross or X it to the ballside, the defense will become very conscious of the cutter to the low-post area. They may front or at least deny the post in a three-quarters position (see (4) in Diagram 3-6).

This often permits (2) to pass to the high-post cutter (5). Once (5) receives the ball, the post may shoot, pass inside to (4) on a partner option, or reverse the ball to (1) in the offside wing position. See Diagram 3-7.

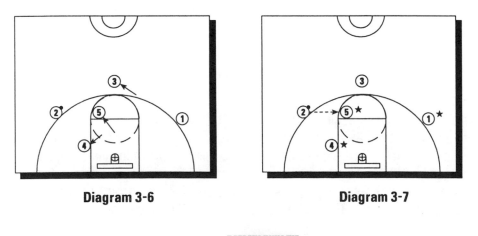

Diagram 3-6

Diagram 3-7

Once the ball is returned to a perimeter player, the basic pattern may be resumed.

If (2) cannot make the pass to (5) or (4), (2) passes to (3) at the point. Player (3) then passes to a wing to resume the motion. In Diagram 3-8, (3) chooses to pass to (1) and then loops down and around (4) and (5). This tells (4) and (5) to move to the ballside and (2) to replace the point position. See Diagram 3-9.

Player (1) can then pass to (4) or (5), or quickly reverse the ball to (3) by way of (2).

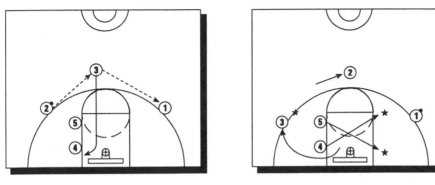

Crossing Post Entry
Diagram 3-8

Posts X It
Diagram 3-9

Strongside Pass and Pop the Stack

If the point (3) in Diagram 3-10, chooses to pass to the strongside wing (2), the two post players may simply post up or pop the stack. They pop the stack when high post (5) screens down for the low post (4), who pops to the high-post position. The perimeter players make a pass-and-move-away maneuver.

If this does not result in a post player being open, the basic weakside motion may be resumed. See Diagram 3-11.

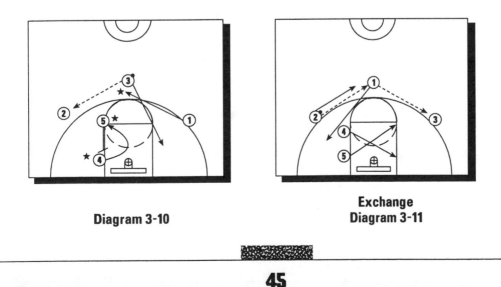

Diagram 3-10

Exchange
Diagram 3-11

Corner Lob Option

During the basic pattern, the ballside low-post player has the option of cutting to the corner or short corner. In Diagram 3-12, (5) cuts to the corner to create an overload and (1) passes to (4).

This keys high post (5) to drop down to the low-post area for a possible pass from (4) (post-to-post pass). Also note that (3), in the offside wing area, was aware of the overload and assumed a rebounding position. See Diagram 3-13.

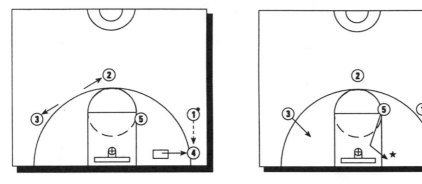

Diagram 3-12   **Diagram 3-13**

If (5) is not open in the cut to the low post, the ball is passed to (2) at the point by way of (1). Player (2) then takes a dribble toward (3), who moves up to a position at the free throw line extended. During this time, (5) has moved out to screen the defender, who guarded (4) in the corner. Player (4) cuts off (5)'s screen, and (2) may lob to (4). See Diagrams 3-14 and 3-15.

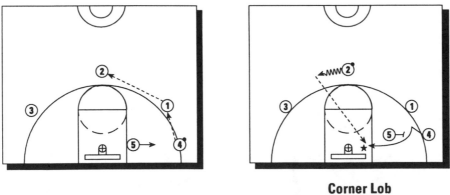

Diagram 3-14

**Corner Lob
Diagram 3-15**

If (4) is not open, (4) assumes the low post and (5) cuts back to the high post. See Diagram 3-16. The motion resumes as (2) passes to (3) and exchanges with (1). Players (4) and (5) then cross to the ballside. See Diagram 3-17.

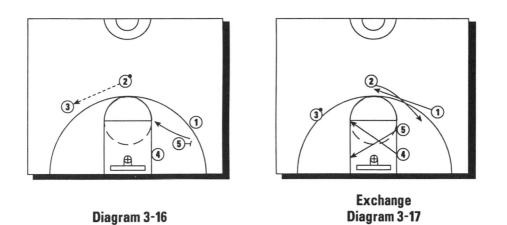

Diagram 3-16

Exchange
Diagram 3-17

Auxiliary Plays

In most situations, the basic zone crossing-post offensive pattern that has been presented is sufficient. However, when additional play action is desired, one of the following auxiliary plays may be considered.

Basic Motion from a Two-Player Front

If the point guard (1) lacks the ability to bring the ball upcourt with little or no help, (2) may assist the point. The offense then starts in a 2-3 shape until the first guard-to-forward pass is made. Diagram 3-18 shows the pass being made to the weakside (away from post (5)). This tells (1) to cross to the offside wing area as forward (4) cuts to the ballside low-post area. Player (5) then cuts to the ballside high-post area and the basic pattern set is aligned. See Diagram 3-19.

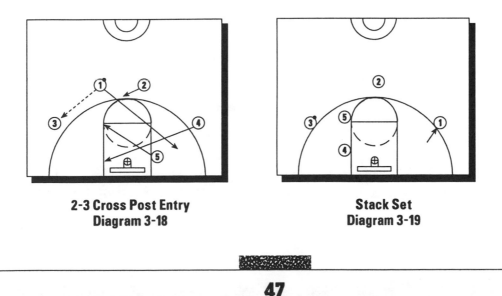

2-3 Cross Post Entry
Diagram 3-18

Stack Set
Diagram 3-19

When the pass is made to the strongside forward, (4) in Diagram 3-20, the guard who made the pass, (2), again crosses to the offside wing position as forward (3) cuts to the ballside high-post area. The team is then in the basic pattern set. See Diagram 3-21.

In order for this play to be functional, (3) must be able to play inside and (4) must be an adequate perimeter player.

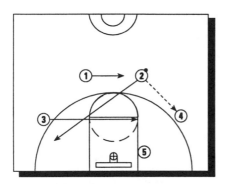
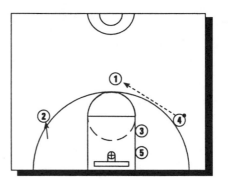

2-3 Cross Post Entry
Diagram 3-20

Diagram 3-21

Shuffle Cross

Another way to start the basic motion from a 2-1-2 set is the shuffle cross. This method is utilized by many shuffle teams to get into the pinwheel shuffle. It is used in this case to allow (2) to help (1) bring the ball upcourt and initiate the offense. Diagram 3-22 shows (1) and (2) in the guard positions, post (5) in the high-post area, and (3) and (4) assuming forward positions at the free throw line extended.

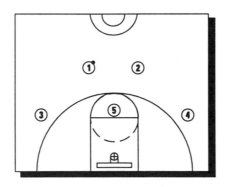

Diagram 3-22

Player (1) passes to (3) and cuts in front of (2) to screen for the offside forward (4). Player (2) uses (1)'s cut to move to the ballside low-post position; and (4) cuts to the point. See Diagram 3-23.

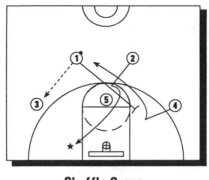

Shuffle Cross
Diagram 3-23

Post (5) swings to the ballside high post and the team is set to run the basic pattern. See Diagrams 3-24 and 3-25.

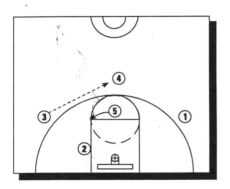

Diagram 3-24

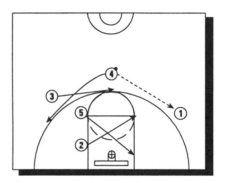

Cross Post with Exchange
Diagram 3-25

This method of initiating the offense is based on the assumption that (4) can play the perimeter, and (2) can operate inside.

Wing-Inside Play

As point (1) passes to weakside wing (2), the offside wing (3) cuts over high post (4), and to the ballside low-post area. See Diagram 3-26.

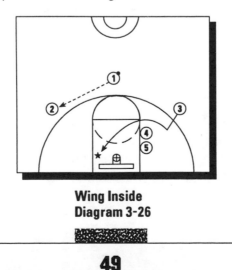

Wing Inside
Diagram 3-26

Player (3) will probably not be open on this cut but (5) now has two options that add variety to the basic offense. Player (5) may:

(A) Swing to the ballside high-post area. See Diagram 3-27. This tells (4) to screen the nearest zone player on the offside of (1). Player (1) moves to the offside wing for a possible lob pass from (2); (4) then pops to the point. See Diagram 3-28.

   If (1) is not open, the motion resumes with (3) as an inside man and (4) as a perimeter player. See Diagram 3-29.

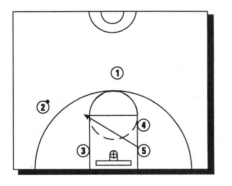

Diagram 3-27

Second Side Lob
Diagram 3-28

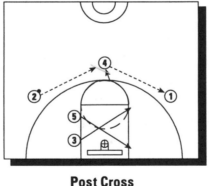

Post Cross
Diagram 3-29

(B) Or if the low post pops out, (5) may decide not to swing across the lane. When this happens, (2) reverses the ball back by way of (1) and (5) pops out of (4)'s downscreen for a possible shot. See Diagram 3-30.

   If (5) does not have a shot, (3) swings back to the ballside high-post position and the motion resumes with (3) as an inside player and (5) as a perimeter player. See Diagram 3-31.

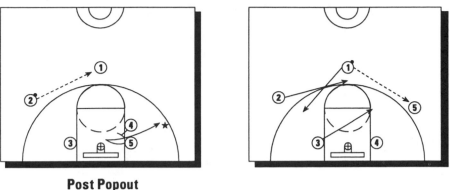

Post Popout
Diagram 3-30

Diagram 3-31

This play is also based on the assumption that (3) has the ability and size to play inside and (4) and (5) can play the perimeter.

Weakside Dribble Entry

While the basic motion is progressing, the player at the point, (1) in Diagram 3-32, may dribble at the weakside wing and clear that player across the lane or back to the point in a "loop" option.

Wing (2) takes the point when (3) goes through and the ball is quickly reversed to (3) for a jump shot. Players (4) and (5) comprise a double screen that disallows the zone to get out to (3). See Diagram 3-33.

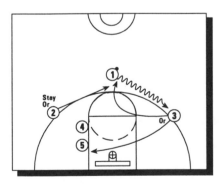

Weakside Dribble Entry
Diagram 3-32

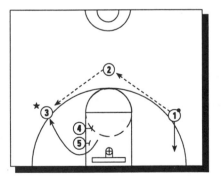

Diagram 3-33

Note that after passing to (2) at the point, (1) dropped low. Very often the defense will visually recognize the potential of the double screen for (3) and overshift to a degree that (1) is left wide open. So it is sometimes a functional move for (2) to fake a pass to (3) behind the double screen and then pass back to (1). See Diagram 3-34.

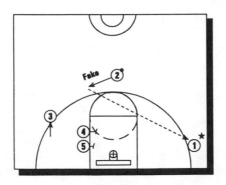

Diagram 3-34

Strongside Dribble-Entry Play

Diagram 3-35 shows point (1) dribbling at the strongside wing (2). This clears (2) down to loop around the two post players (4) and (5) and to the point. It also tells the offside wing (3) to cut to the ballside corner.

This movement creates an overload that is utilized by moving the ball around the passing triangles. See Diagram 3-36.

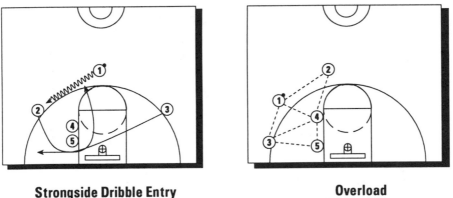

Strongside Dribble Entry
Diagram 3-35

Overload
Diagram 3-36

A Balancing Move

The overload is maintained until wing (1) decides to change it. (1) may do this by passing to (2) and cutting over the post players to the offside wing area. Player (3) then replaces (1) at the wing. This balances the offense and the basic motion may be resumed. See Diagram 3-37.

Diagram 3-37

Fake Balancing Move

When (1) was at the wing and passed to (2) at the point, (1) could have faked the balancing move and cut over the posts and back to the ballside corner. Player (3) could again replace (1) at the wing, thus forming a new overload formation. See Diagrams 3-38 and 3-39.

This maneuver very often results in (1) being open in the corner. If no shot is forthcoming, it would be up to new wing (3) to change the overload.

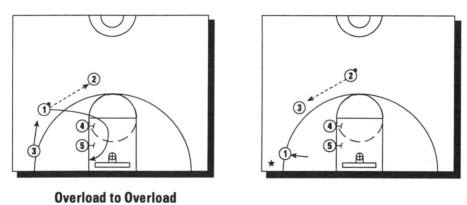

Overload to Overload
Diagram 3-38

Diagram 3-39

High-Post-to-the-Point Series

This series is keyed by point (1) passing to the weakside wing, (2) in Diagram 3-40, and instead of cutting away from the pass, cutting to the ballside corner. This cut tells the two post players to make their crossing action with (4) (the player cutting to the high post) going all the way to the point. See (4) in Diagram 3-40.

This movement creates an overload with (4) at the point. The new four-player perimeter tends to spread the zone and may leave (5) open inside the defense. See Diagram 3-41.

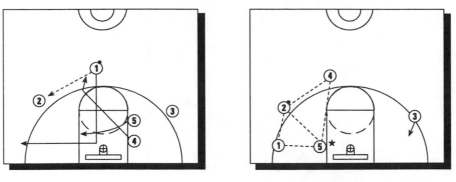

Diagram 3-40   **Diagram 3-41**

The overload triangles are then utilized until (2), the strongside wing, decides to change the overload. The wing can do this by passing to (4) at the point and cutting to the far corner. Player (4) then passes to (3), and (4) and (5) make their crossing motion to the ballside of the lane with (5) assuming the point. Player (1) replaces (2) at the wing. See Diagram 3-42.

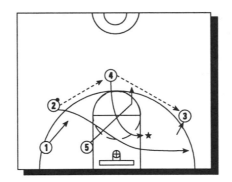

Diagram 3-42

This action fits very well with the basic motion because the point player's cut to the ballside corner is an obvious key. In all other cases, the point cuts away from the entry pass.

Zone Backdoor Play

At the point in the basic zone motion where the low post cuts to the corner, a backdoor play may be used. In Diagram 3-43, low post (5) cuts to the corner as the ball is passed from point (1) to wing (2). Player (1) then cuts away and is replaced at the point by (3).

Player (2) fakes a pass to (5) in the corner to draw a defender to (5). Hopefully at this point there is a defender on (5) in the corner, the trailing inside defensive player is guarding (4), and the third inside defender is across the lane. See Diagram 3-44.

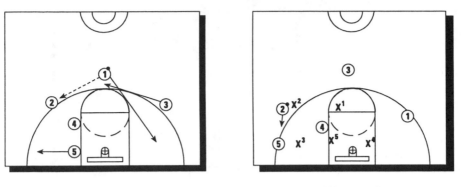

Diagram 3-43 **Diagram 3-44**

Player (4) takes a step up to receive a pass from (2); (2) passes to (4) and exchanges with (3) at the point. The motion of (2) screening for (3) and (3) cutting to the wing occupies the defender on (5), thus allowing (5) to make an unmolested backdoor cut to the ballside lay-up slot. See Diagram 3-45.

If the inside defender across the lane attempts to help out, (1) may be open on the offside. See Diagram 3-46. Player (4) should be taught to catch the ball, pivot toward and face the basket, and throw a two-hand overhead pass to (5), or to (1). If neither is open, (4) passes to (3), and the basic motion is resumed.

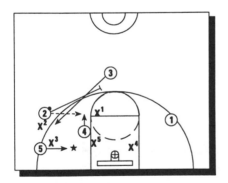

Post Backdoor
Diagram 3-45

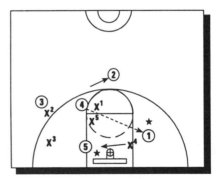

Diagram 3-46

Crossing Posts from a 2-3 Set
If a team desires to run from a 2-3 set, a pattern very similar to the basic crossing post zone offense may be run. Diagram 3-47 shows the personnel alignment with players (1) and (2) in the guard positions, (3) playing the baseline roamer, and big players (4) and (5) in the post positions.

The motion begins as guard (1) dribbles toward the baseline roamer (3). Player (1) passes to (3) and cuts away to be replaced by the other guard (2). See Diagram 3-48.

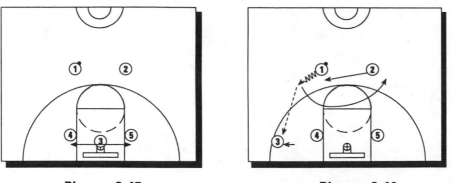

Diagram 3-47   **Diagram 3-48**

Players (3), (2), and (4) then utilize the overload triangle as (5) cuts to the ballside high-post area. Player (1) becomes the offside rebounder by finishing the loop as high as the free throw line. See Diagram 3-49.

From there, the standard crossing post options would prevail. Player (3) may pass to (5), who could shoot or pass inside to (4). See Diagram 3-50. Player (3) could also pass to (2) and change the overload by cutting to the far corner. See Diagram 3-51 and 3-52.

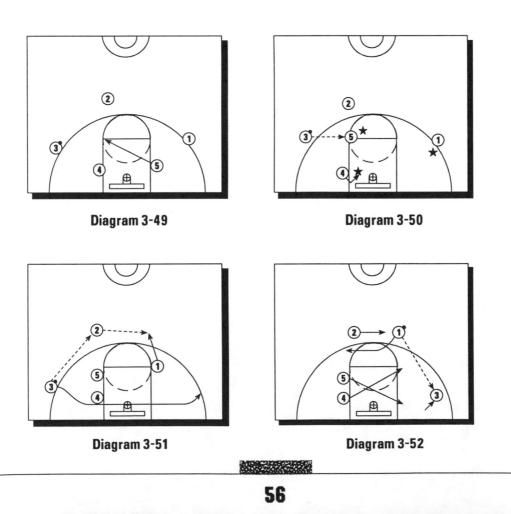

Diagram 3-49   **Diagram 3-50**

Diagram 3-51   **Diagram 3-52**

Note: On (1)'s initial cut to start the play, (1) could have utilized either of the other two pass-and-move-away cuts. (1) could have cut down and around the offside low post (5). See Diagram 3-53.

Player (1) could also have used an offside screen by (2) to cut away for a possible lob pass. See Diagram 3-54.

From there, the options for (3) are the same as before.

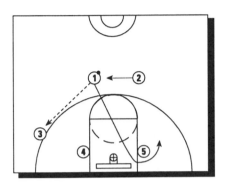

Guard Through to Post Pinch
Diagram 3-53

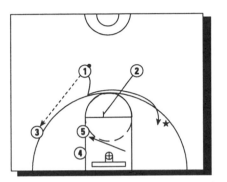

Second Side Lob
Diagram 3-54

Popping the Stack

When (3) chooses to keep the ball on the same side and utilize the passing triangles, the posts may create ballside motion by popping the stack. This maneuver is keyed by the high post, (5) in Diagram 3-55, who screens down for the low post (4), who pops to the high post area. This motion may result in either post getting open.

This alignment is then maintained until (3) passes to (2) and cuts to the offside corner.

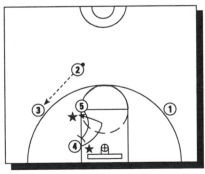

Diagram 3-55

Three-Crossing-Posts Set

If players (3), (4), and (5) are of equal strength on the boards, and in terms of outside shooting ability, the inside rotation may be a three-player motion, much like Dean Smith's T Game. Diagram 3-56 shows (1) passing to (3) and making a loop cut, and (5) cutting to the ballside high-post area.

When the ball is reversed as shown in Diagram 3-57, the onside guard (1) dribbles a little deeper as (5) and (4) cut to the ballside. Player (3) takes the offside low-post area. See Diagram 3-58.

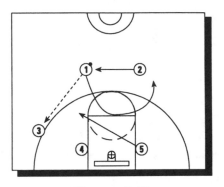

Diagram 3-56

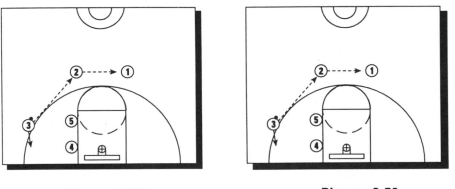

Diagram 3-57   **Diagram 3-58**

If neither (5) nor (4) is open, (5) clears to the corner, (4) drops low, and (3) cuts to the ballside high post. See Diagram 3-59.

Once (1) passes to (5), (1) exchanges with (2) on a loop cut and the same options prevail. See Diagram 3-60.

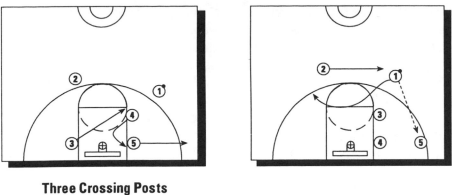

Three Crossing Posts
Diagram 3-59

Diagram 3-60

This time, however, the decision to switch the overload is up to the ballside guard ((2) in Diagram 3-61). Player (2) may utilize the ballside passing triangle (see Diagram 3-61), pass to a post (see Diagram 3-62), or switch the overload by passing to (1) (see Diagrams 3-63 and 3-64).

Both these methods test the zone by overloading it and attempting to penetrate it by passing to a post man.

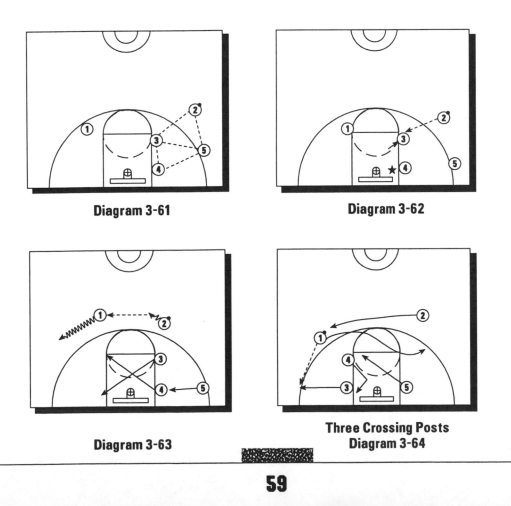

Diagram 3-61

Diagram 3-62

Diagram 3-63

Three Crossing Posts
Diagram 3-64

This Crossing-Post Zone Offense thoroughly tests the zone defense. It probes the zone's middle, tests its corner, overloads and overshifts it, screens the offside, and provides an offside lob option. The players can best take advantage of their talents because big players (4) and (5) usually remain close to the basket, and mobile players (1), (2), and (3) test the zone's perimeter with a variety of pass-and-move-away maneuvers. All in all, this offense is a comprehensive zone plan that should provide an abundance of high-percentage shots. It must be pointed out that the heart of this offense is the basic motion. Auxiliary plays are added only when and if needed. Too much motion against a zone can be detrimental.

CHAPTER 4

The Guard Deep Loop Zone Offense

The Guard Deep Loop Zone Offense contains many fundamental zone maneuvers. It has a changing perimeter that causes problems for adjusting zones, tests the middle of the zone, tests the corners, provides excellent rebounding opportunities, and may be set in a variety of manners that facilitate different personnel alignments.

The 2-3 Set Personnel Alignment

When run from a 2-3 set, this offense is designed for one small lead guard (1), three interchangeable players, (2), (3), and (4), who should have adequate size and good ballhandling skills, and a strong post player (5), who should be a rebounder able to score with his or her back to the basket. See Diagram 4-1.

As guards (1) and (2) bring the ball upcourt, they should be positioned at least as wide as the free throw lane; (3) and (4) are as high as the free throw line extended and at a wide forward position. Post (5) is on (1)'s side of the court.

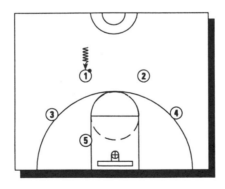

Diagram 4-1

The Basic Pattern

The basic pattern from a 2-3 set begins as (1) passes to (2) who passes to (4). Player (2) then cuts down and around post (5). See Diagram 4-2. It may seem odd to have (1) bring the ball up and pass to (2) before (2) makes the key penetration pass to (4). However, this pass will often freeze an adjusting zone in a two-player front, and it allows the offense to split it once (2) cuts through on a deep loop cut. It is also advantageous to have (1), the point-type guard, bring the ball upcourt.

As soon as (2) clears the lane, the offside forward (3) cuts to the high-post area, looking for a pass from (4). When this pass is made, (3) can shoot, look inside the zone for (5), who might be open for a power lay-up shot, or reverse the ball to (2), looping around (5). See Diagram 4-3. See Diagram 4-6. (5) screens for (2), steps up to the ball (3), and posts up if (2) receives a pass.

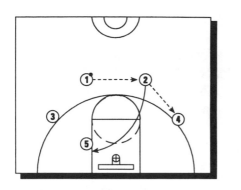

Guard Deep Loop
Diagram 4-2

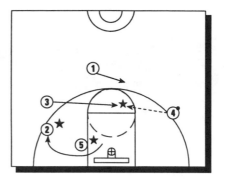

Diagram 4-3

If (4) cannot make the pass to (3), (4) passes to (1), who comes to meet the ball. Player (1) then reverses the ball to (2), looping around (5). It is important that (2) learns to maintain balance as he or she cuts around (5), then looks up immediately, and catches the ball in an all-purpose triple-threat position. Player (3) then slides down to the open low-post position to clear the way for (4) to cut into the high-post area. See Diagram 4-4.

Player (2) may shoot, pass to (4) in the high-post area, who could shoot or look inside for either (5) or (3). Player (2) also may pass directly inside to post (5), who is "posting up."

If these options do not produce a shot, (2) dribbles out front and the offense is reset with (1) moving across the lane, (4) occupying the ballside forward slot, (3) moving up to a position at the free throw line extended, and (5) moving across the lane to be on (1)'s side of the court. See Diagram 4-5.

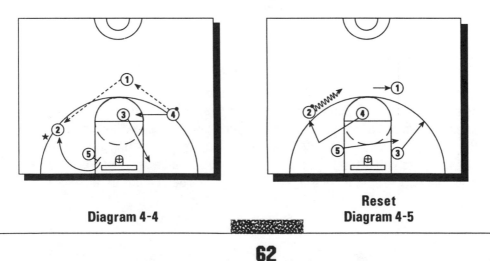

Diagram 4-4

Reset
Diagram 4-5

This returns the offense to a two-player front from which the basic pattern can be run. Player (2) would pass to (1), receive a return pass, pass to (4), and make the guard-deep-loop cut that keys the pattern.

Guard Deep Loop
Diagram 4-6

Overload Phase

This phase of the offense is keyed by (1), the strongside guard, who passes to forward (3). This tells (2), the offside guard, to cut down and around (5) and to the ballside corner to form an overload. See Diagram 4-7.

From there, the overload is utilized as the ball is passed around the triangles formed by (1), (3), (2), and (5). It is important at this time for (4), the offside forward, to drop low and assume a rebounding position. See Diagram 4-8.

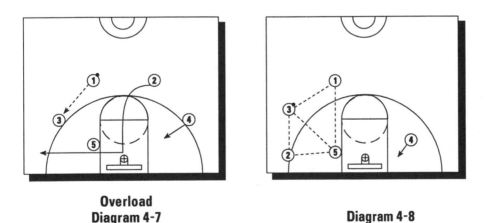

Overload
Diagram 4-7

Diagram 4-8

This overload is maintained until (1) reverses the ball to (4). Once this happens, (3) cuts to the high-post area and (2) replaces (3) at the wing position. If (4) passes to (3), (3) may shoot, look inside for (5), or reverse the ball to (2). See Diagram 4-9.

If (4) cannot pass to (3), he or she reverses the ball to (2) by way of (1). This tells (3) to drop low and (4) to cut to the high-post area. See Diagram 4-10.

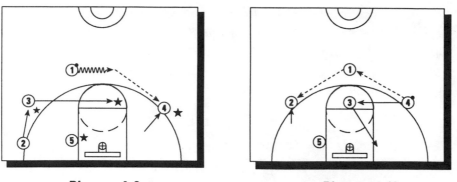

Diagram 4-9   Diagram 4-10

If (2) can get the ball to (4) at the apex of the triangle, (4) may shoot, or pass to the players that form the base, either (5) or (3). See Diagram 4-11.

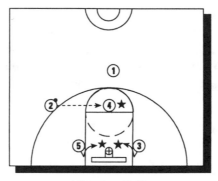

Diagram 4-11

Low-Cut Lob Play from the 2-3 Set

The basic pattern may also be run to provide an offside lob pass. The motion starts as before with (2) passing to forward (3), and cutting down and around the post (5) on the far side of the lane. See Diagram 4-12.

This time, however, the offside forward (4) does not cut to the high post. Instead, (4) cuts low and moves across the lane. If timed correctly, this cut can provide (2) with a double screen as he or she moves around (5). See Diagram 4-13.

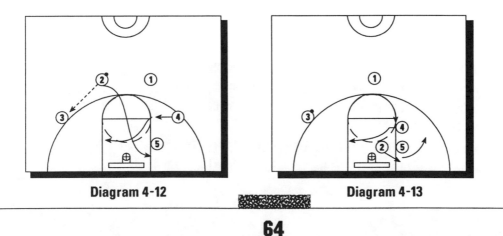

Diagram 4-12   Diagram 4-13

Player (3) then reverses the ball to (2) by way of (1). See Diagram 4-14.

If (2) is not open, (4) continues across the lane and screens for (3). Player (2) looks at (3) for a possible crosscourt lob pass. See Diagram 4-15.

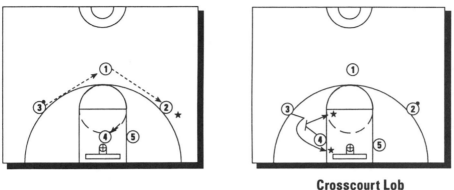

Diagram 4-14

Crosscourt Lob
Diagram 4-15

If (3) is not open, he or she crosses the lane to the ballside corner. Player (2) may then: (A) utilize the overload passing triangles (see Diagram 4-16), (B) reverse the ball to (4) and cut to the middle (see Diagram 4-17), or (C) dribble out front to put the offense back in a two-player front. See Diagram 4-18.

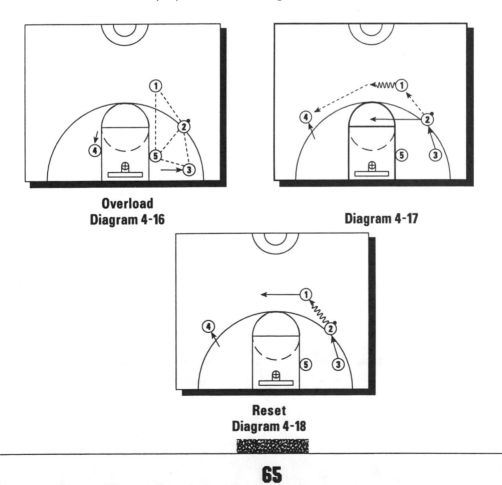

Overload
Diagram 4-16

Diagram 4-17

Reset
Diagram 4-18

High Post-Out Set (1-3-1 to 2-3)

This method allows a team that features a very basic 1-3-1 attack with little motion to quickly convert to a 2-3 set, run a pattern, and, if desired, return to the 1-3-1 formation.

1-3-1 to 2-3 Adjustment

Diagram 4-19 shows the team in a 1-3-1 set with (1) at the point, (2) and (3) at the wings, (4) at the high post, and (5) as the baseline roamer.

Player (1) keys the high-post-out 2-3 set by dribbling away from baseline roamer (5)'s side. This dribble tells high post (4) to pop out to the offside guard position. See Diagram 4-20.

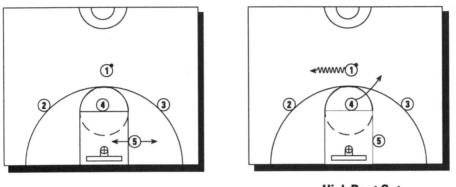

Diagram 4-19

High Post Out
Diagram 4-20

Player (1) then passes to (4) to remind the other players that the adjustment to a 2-3 set has been made. See Diagram 4-21. (1) gets a return pass from (4), passes to the wing on the side (2), and cuts down around (5). See Diagram 4-22.

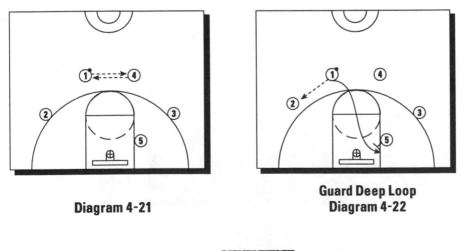

Diagram 4-21

Guard Deep Loop
Diagram 4-22

This keys the offside forward (3) to cut to the high post area. If (3) is open, (2) passes to (3), who can shoot, look inside for (5), or reverse the ball to (1). See Diagram 4-23.

If (2) cannot pass to (3), (3) drops low and (2) reverses the ball to (1) by way of (4). See Diagram 4-24.

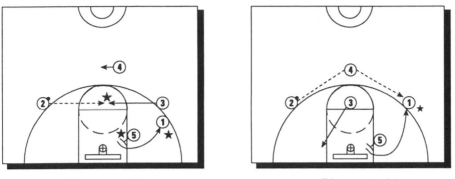

| **Diagram 4-23** | **Diagram 4-24** |

Once (1) receives the ball, (2) cuts to the high post area and (1) may pass to (2) for the triangle options (see Diagram 4-25) or (as shown in Diagram 4-26) dribble out front to reset the offense.

Please note that (4) had the option of staying out front to run a new pattern or returning to the high post to set the team in a 1-3-1 formation.

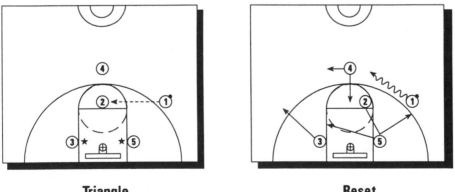

| **Triangle** | **Reset** |
| **Diagram 4-25** | **Diagram 4-26** |

Low-Cut Lob-Pass Play

Diagram 4-27 shows (1) again dribbling opposite baseline roamer (5). This calls (4) out front. Player (1) passes to (4) and gets a return pass. Player (1) then passes to forward (2) and cuts down and around post (5). See Diagram 4-28.

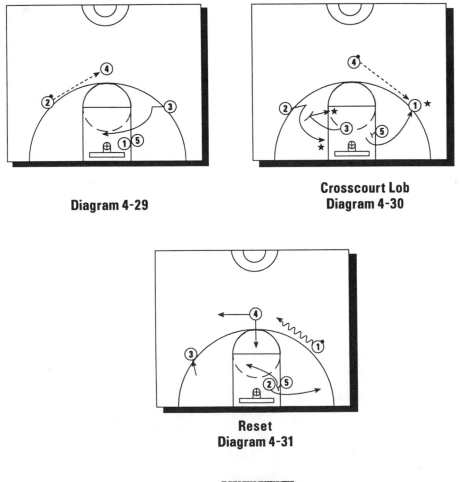

High Post Out
Diagram 4-27

Diagram 4-28

This time, however, (3) chooses to cut low instead of to the high-post area. This calls the lob-pass play. Player (2) quickly passes to (4), and (3) crosses the lane (see Diagram 4-29). At this point, (4) must time the pass to give (3) time to screen for (2). Player (4) then passes to (1), who may shoot, lob crosscourt to (2) (see Diagram 4-30), or dribble out front to reset the offense (see Diagram 4-31).

Diagram 4-29

Crosscourt Lob
Diagram 4-30

Reset
Diagram 4-31

Again note that (4) had the option of returning to the high-post area and calling the 1-3-1 offense or calling for a 2-3 pattern by moving to the offside guard position.

The Basic Motion From a 1-2-2 Set

Personnel Alignment

If a team desires to run its zone offense from a 1-2-2 set, a similar pattern may be run. Diagram 4-32 shows a point guard (1), two wing players, (2) and (3), and two post players, (4) and (5).

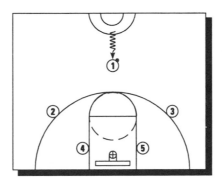

Diagram 4-32

The Basic Motion

The pattern begins as point (1) passes to a wing (as to (2) in Diagram 4-33). This tells the offside wing (3) to cut to the high-post area for a pass from (2) and a possible triangle play with (4) and (5).

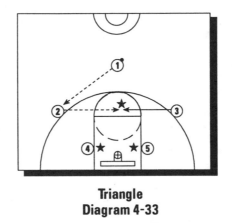

Triangle
Diagram 4-33

If (3) is not open, he or she continues to the ballside corner to form an overload on that side. The overload passing triangles are then used until the ballside wing (2) decides to change it. See Diagram 4-34. Player (2) does this by passing to point (1) and cutting over (4) and under (5) to the offside wing. Player (3) moves up to replace (2) at the wing. See Diagram 4-35.

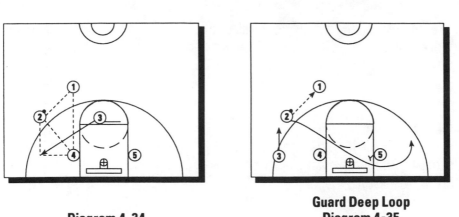

Diagram 4-34

Guard Deep Loop
Diagram 4-35

In order for (1) to time the reversal pass to (2), he or she may pass to (3), receive a return pass, and then pass to (2). See Diagram 4-36.

Player (1) should at least fake to (3) and then dribble to (2)'s side and make the pass. See Diagram 4-37.

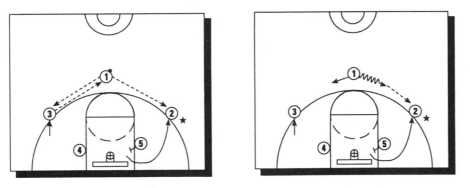

Diagram 4-36

Diagram 4-37

Once the pass is made to (2), the offside wing (3) cuts to the middle and the same options will prevail. See Diagram 4-38 through 4-42.

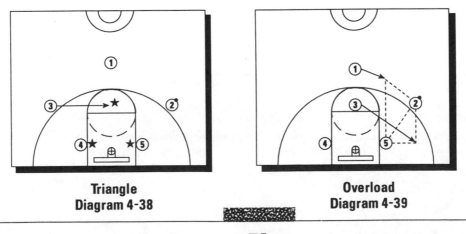

Triangle
Diagram 4-38

Overload
Diagram 4-39

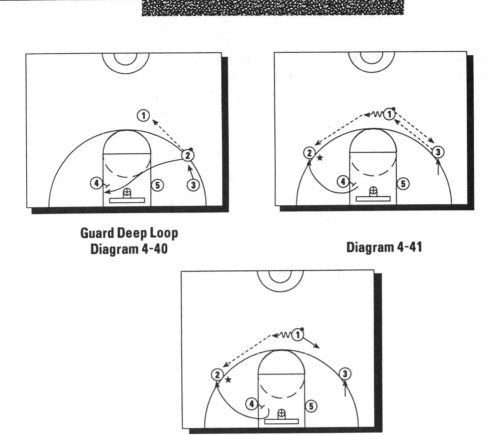

Guard Deep Loop
Diagram 4-40

Diagram 4-41

Diagram 4-42

Low-Cut Lob Play from the 1-2-2 Set

When running the low-cut lob play, (1) passes to a wing (as to (2) in Diagram 4-43) and gets a quick return pass. This or a verbal call tells the onside post (4) to move up to screen for (2).

Player (1) quickly passes the ball to (3); (2) makes a fake to the high post area and cuts off (4) for a possible lob pass from (3). See Diagram 4-44.

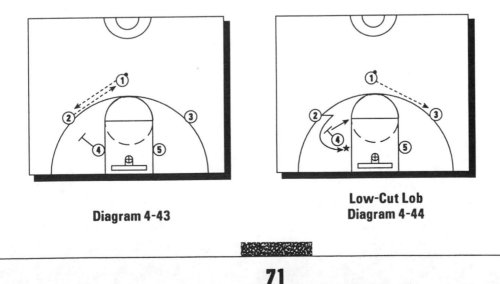

Diagram 4-43

Low-Cut Lob
Diagram 4-44

If (2) is not open for the lob pass, he or she continues across the lane to the ballside corner. Player (3) may then utilize the overload passing triangles (see Diagram 4-45) or pass the ball to (1) and balance the offense. See Diagrams 4-46 and 4-47.

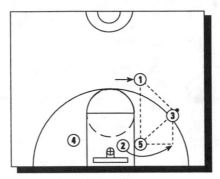

Triangle
Diagram 4-45

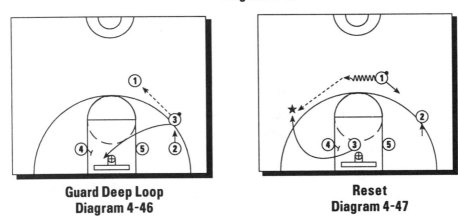

Guard Deep Loop
Diagram 4-46

Reset
Diagram 4-47

Auxiliary Plays

Weakside Dribble Entry from the 2-3 Set

In Diagram 4-48, the weakside guard (2) dribbles at forward (4) and clears that player across the lane. As soon as (2) picks up the dribble, the offside forward (3) cuts to the high-post area. When (2) dribble chases (4), (4) may choose to loop cut back to (2)'s original position.

Diagram 4-48

Player (2) may then pass to (3) in the middle, who may shoot, pass inside to (5), or reverse the ball to (4), who loops around pinch-post (5). See Diagram 4-49. Player (2) also has the option of reversing the ball to (4) by way of (1). See Diagram 4-50. Player (3) clears low and (2) cuts to the middle. See Diagram 4-51.

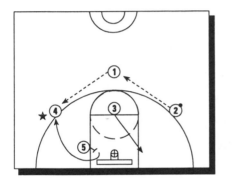

Diagram 4-50

Diagram 4-51

Strongside Dribble Entry from the 2-3 Set

This time, the strongside guard (1) dribbles at forward (3) and clears (3) across the lane. This tells the offside forward (4) to screen down for (3); (3) loops around (4) as (1) reverses the ball to (3) by way of (2). See Diagram 4-52.

Player (1) then cuts to the middle for a triangle play. See Diagram 4-53.

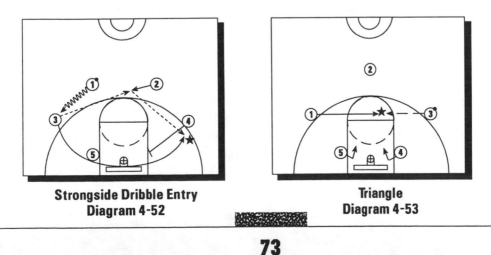

Strongside Dribble Entry
Diagram 4-52

Triangle
Diagram 4-53

If (3) cannot get the ball to (1), (4) clears across the lane and loops around (5). Player (3) reverses the ball to (4) by way of (2). See Diagram 4-54.

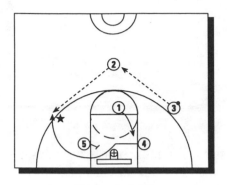

Diagram 4-54

Double Stack Play from the 2-3 Set

The double stack maneuver usually isn't thought of as a zone play, but actually it creates many problems for a zone defense. The downscreens of the two post players (as by (4) and (5) in Diagram 4-55) tend to trap the zone inside, as the two wings, (2) and (3), pop to their wing positions. These screens and cuts may also spread the zone and leave one of the two post players open inside if the defenders fight over the downscreens. Post players (4) and (5) screen, step up, and post up as the cutters use their screens. See Diagram 4-56.

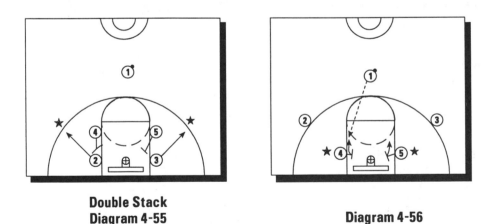

**Double Stack
Diagram 4-55**

Diagram 4-56

The double stack play that is interjected into the basic 2-3 pattern must be keyed by a hand signal because it looks very much like the low-cut lob play. In Diagram 4-57, (2) passes to (4) and cuts through. Ordinarily this would key (3) to cut to the high-post area. This time, however, (3) cuts low under post (5). Player (4) passes to (1) and screens down for (3). Since (2) is looping under (5), the net result is a double stack maneuver. See Diagram 4-58.

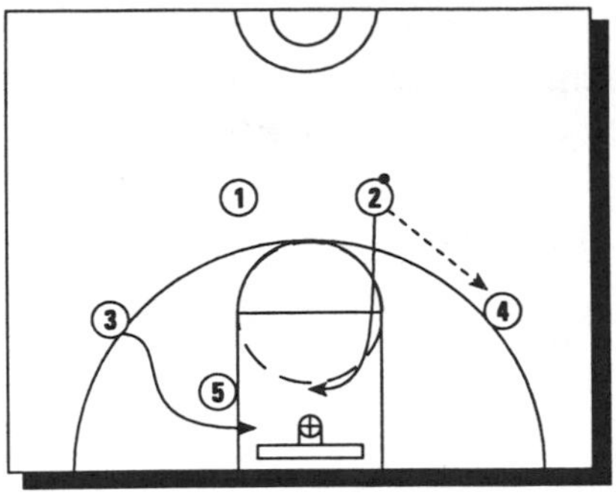

Diagram 4-57

Double Stack
Diagram 4-58

Once (1) passes to either wing (as to (2) in Diagram 4-59), the offside wing cuts to the middle and the pattern is resumed. See Diagrams 4-60 and 4-61.

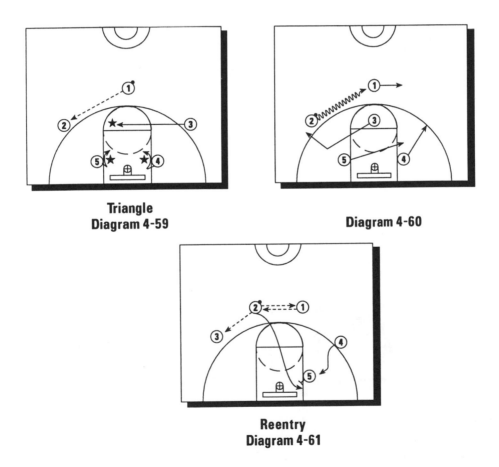

Triangle
Diagram 4-59

Diagram 4-60

Reentry
Diagram 4-61

Strongside Guard-Through from the 2-3 Set

Ordinarily, the weakside guard (2) initiates the basic play by passing to the weakside forward (4) and then cutting down and around post (5). See Diagram 4-62.

When running the weakside guard loop play, (1) passes to forward (3) and cuts down to key the weakside forward (4) to screen down and trap the zone inside. See Diagram 4-63.

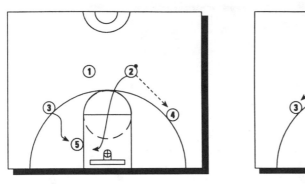

Diagram 4-62

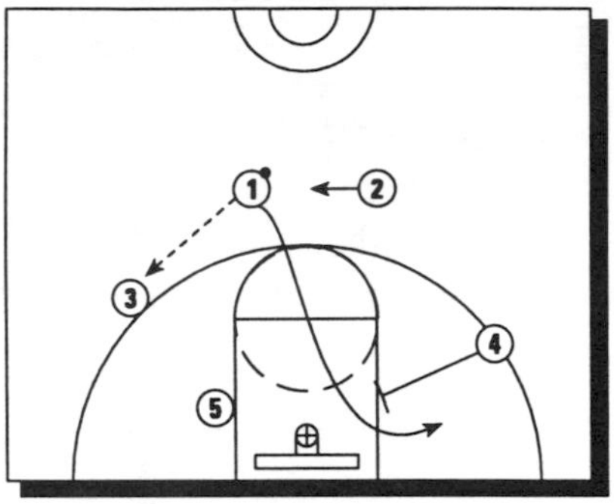

Strongside Guard-Through
Diagram 4-63

Player (3) then reverses the ball to (1) by way of the point (2). See Diagram 4-64. Player (1) then shoots, looks for (3) cutting to the middle (see Diagram 4-65), or reverses the ball to (4), who has crossed the lane and looped around post (5). See Diagram 4-66.

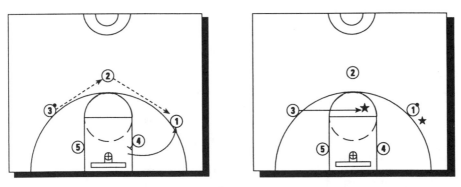

Diagram 4-64

Triangle
Diagram 4-65

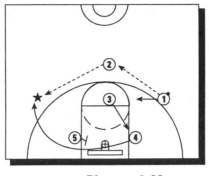

Diagram 4-66

Double-Screen Play from the 2-3 Set

This play is also similar to the low-cut lob play and should be keyed with a hand or verbal signal. If (2) is a strong jump shooter, the double-screen play may be added. Diagram 4-67 shows (2) passing to forward (4) and making a cut down and around post (5). This time, however, (3), instead of cutting to the high-post area, moves down and joins (5) to form a double screen or wall. Player (2) loops around this wall and the ball is reversed to (2) by way of (1). The zone is caught overshifted and trapped inside by the double screen. See Diagram 4-68.

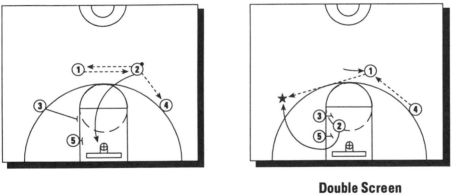

Diagram 4-67

Double Screen
Diagram 4-68

If (2) is not open, (3) continues across the lane and (4) cuts to the middle to resume the pattern. See Diagrams 4-69 and 4-70.

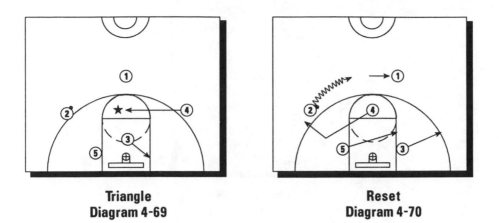

Triangle
Diagram 4-69

Reset
Diagram 4-70

The Guard-Deep-Loop Offense will permit your team to present an ever-changing perimeter, overshift and overload the zone, get the ball inside, and test its middle and corner. Pick a set that best fits your personnel and start with just the basic pattern. Do not be in a hurry to add extra plays unless it is absolutely necessary. Once your players become comfortable with the pattern, this plan will provide a winning zone offense.

CHAPTER 5

An Inside-Oriented Zone Offense

Perhaps the first consideration in choosing an offense is deciding if it fits the talents of your players. The following plan illustrates that truism and is designed for a team seeking an inside-oriented zone offense. This would be a team with questionable outside shooting ability and strong inside capabilities. This offense provides opportunities for many inside shots and features rebound triangles that lead to second-shot opportunities.

Personnel Alignment

The offense is most often run from a 2-3 set that includes a lead or point guard (1), a large guard (2), a pair of tall post players, (4) and (5), and a single forward (3). See Diagram 5-1.

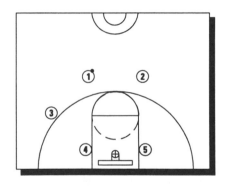

Diagram 5-1

The Basic Pattern

The pattern begins as guard (1) passes to forward (3), and then moves to the offside guard area. This pass keys the offside guard (2) to cut down and to the high-post area. See Diagram 5-2.

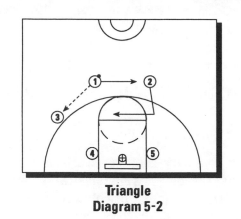
Triangle
Diagram 5-2

Triangle Option
From there (3) should look first for (2). If (2) can get the ball, he or she may shoot or look inside the zone for big players (4) and (5). We call this a triangle play and it places a great deal of pressure on the zone's inside defenders. See Diagram 5-3.

Crosscourt Pass Option
If (3) cannot pass to (2), (3) should look to (1). In most cases, the zone players will be in the positions shown in Diagram 5-4 and (1) may have an unmolested three-point field goal shot.

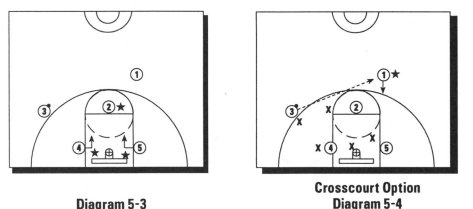

Diagram 5-3

Crosscourt Option
Diagram 5-4

Corner Option
If neither (2) nor (1) is open, the onside big player (4) moves to the ballside corner or short corner. Player (3) then passes to (4) and cuts through. Player (5), the offside big player, uses (3)'s cut as a natural screen to move to the ballside low-post area. See Diagram 5-5.

Please note that throughout most of this pattern, a rebound triangle is maintained. This is very important against zone defenses that wish to hold you to one hurried, outside shot.

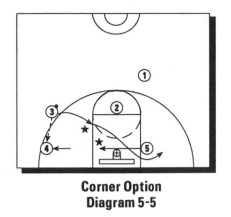

Corner Option
Diagram 5-5

Reverse and Reset Option

If (5) is not open, (2) steps out toward the ballside perimeter and receives a pass from (4). Player (2) then reverses the ball to (1). During this process, posts (4) and (5) return to their original position and (3) moves up to a position at the free throw line extended. See Diagrams 5-6 and 5-7.

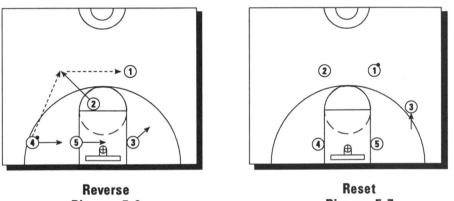

Reverse
Diagram 5-6

Reset
Diagram 5-7

From there, (1) may pass to (3) and repeat the pattern. Note that throughout the pattern, each player is a specialist: (1) stays outside, (2) cuts to the middle, (3) is the lone forward, and (4) and (5) are either inside or corner players.

One-Player-Front Set

If a coach desires to use a one-player-front set for a zone offense, the same motion may be run. This alignment permits the offense to be initiated on either side with a pass from point (1), to a wing and a subsequent cut to the high-post area by the offside wing. It also allows the coach to utilize personnel that includes one small point guard (1), two big players (4) and (5), and wings (2) and (3) who may be tall or short. Diagrams 5-8 through 5-11 show the basic pattern being run from the one-player-front set.

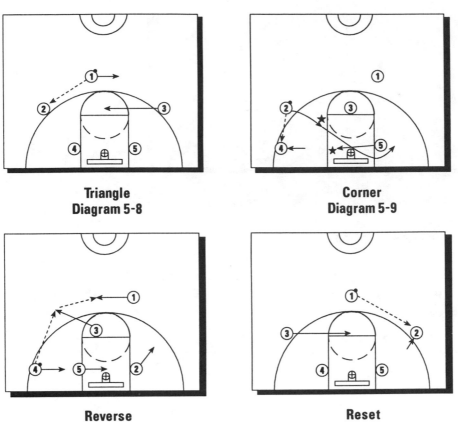

Triangle
Diagram 5-8

Corner
Diagram 5-9

Reverse
Diagram 5-10

Reset
Diagram 5-11

Strong Jump-Shot Variation

If a team has a player (3) who can make a 12- to 15-foot jump shot with consistency, the strong jump-shot variation should be added. Although this variation may be run from either a 2-3 or a 1-2-2 set, we will use the 2-3 set for the purpose of this explanation.

Player (1) passes to (3) and cuts away, and (2) cuts down and to the high post area. See Diagram 5-12.

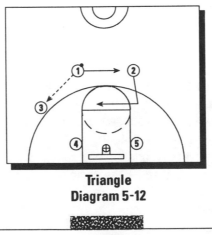

Triangle
Diagram 5-12

Strong Jump-Shooter Variation Key

If nothing develops at this point, (4) cuts to the ballside corner. At this point, (3) keys the jump-shooter variation by passing to (4) and (instead of crossing the lane), (3) "posts up" in the ballside low-post area. See Diagram 5-13. This tells (5) not to come to the ballside.

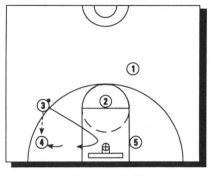

Diagram 5-13

If (4) cannot get the ball to (3), (2) pops to the perimeter and (4) passes to (2), who reverses the ball to (1). See Diagram 5-14.

As (1) receives the ball from (2), (3) times the cut and crosses the lane to loop around (5) and receive the ball for a possible jump shot. See Diagram 5-15.

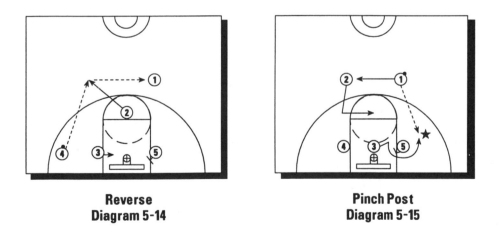

Reverse
Diagram 5-14

Pinch Post
Diagram 5-15

Note that (5) assumed a screening position (screen, step up, post up) and impeded the zone's ability to get out to (3). Also note that as (1) passed to (3), (2) cut to the high post area. This does two things: It provides a rebound triangle in case (3) takes a shot, and if (3) does not shoot, the team is in position to repeat the pattern.

Auxiliary Plays

At this point, the heart of the offense has been presented—the basic pattern, the jump-shot option, and the ability to run the offense from different sets provide a comprehensive zone plan. However, the following auxiliary plays may be used to meet special situations or to give the offense depth as the season progresses.

Stack Play

The stack play is a maneuver that may be added to many zone offenses. It is begun from the 2-3 set, but forward (3) stacks under the ballside post. See Diagram 5-16.

From this alignment, (3) may determine the set that will be run by:

(A) Popping to the point and receiving a pass from (1). Players (1) and (2) then flare to the wings and a 1-2-2 set is run (see Diagram 5-17).

(B) Popping to the wing to form a 2-3 set (see diagram 5-18).

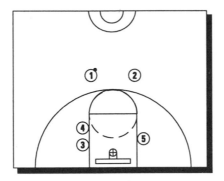

Stack Set
Diagram 5-16

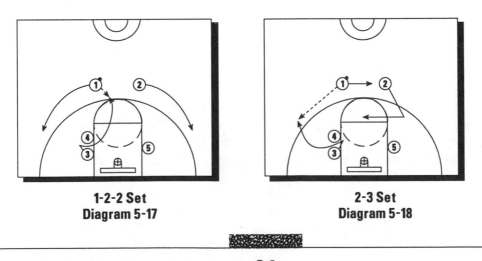

1-2-2 Set   **2-3 Set**
Diagram 5-17   **Diagram 5-18**

This versatility allows (3) to read the defense as the guards bring the ball upcourt, and then make a move that splits the defense and aligns in the gaps. When the defense is in an even-front (2-3 or 2-1-2 zone), (3) pops to the point. See Diagrams 5-19 and 5-20. When the defense is in an odd-front (1-2-2 or 3-2 zone), (3) pops to the wing and again splits the defense in the defensive gaps. See Diagrams 5-21 and 5-22.

Versus an Even Front

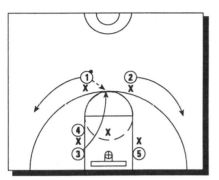

Diagram 5-19

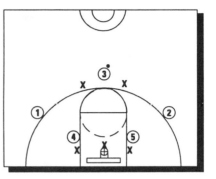

Diagram 5-20

Versus an Odd Front

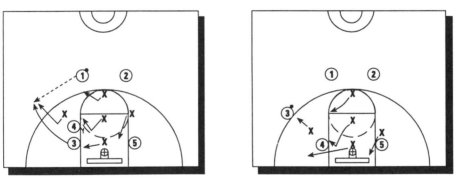

Diagram 5-21

Diagram 5-22

Keying the Pattern Variations Via the Stack Play
The Stack Play may also be used to key the pattern variations. If the inside stacker, (3) in Diagram 5-23, cuts inside, it keys the basic pattern. If (3) chooses to cut to the outside, it keys the strong jump-shooter variation.

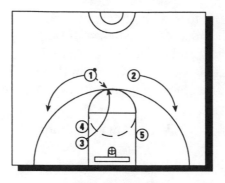

Diagram 5-23

(3) Cuts Inside

Diagrams 5-24 through 5-26 show (3) cut to the inside and key the basic pattern.

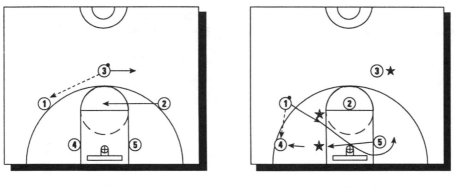

Triangle
Diagram 5-24

Corner
Diagram 5-25

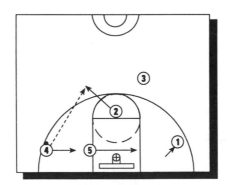

Reverse
Diagram 5-26

(3) Cuts Outside
Diagrams 5-27 through 5-29 show (3) cutting to the outside and keying the strong jump-shooter variation.

This plan allows a team to use both pattern variations, provides definite keys to which pattern is being run, and assures that (3) would get the shot when the strong jump-shooter variation is run.

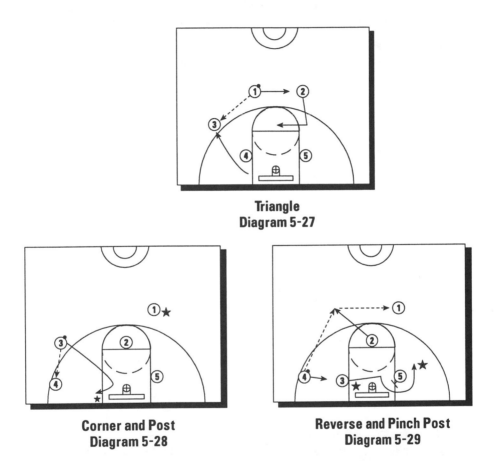

Triangle
Diagram 5-27

Corner and Post
Diagram 5-28

Reverse and Pinch Post
Diagram 5-29

Quick Reverse Play from the 2-3 Set
Once (1) has passed to (3) and (2) has cut to the middle, the quick reverse play may be run. It is keyed by (1), who moves to the ballside and yells "reverse it." Player (3) passes to (1) and this tells post (4) in Diagram 5-30 to clear across the lane and loop around post (5).

Player (1) passes to (4) for a possible jump shot as (5) impedes the path of the zone players attempting to cover (4) (screen, step up, post up). If (4) receives the ball and cannot shoot, (2) drops to the offside low-post area and (3) cuts to the high post. See Diagram 5-31.

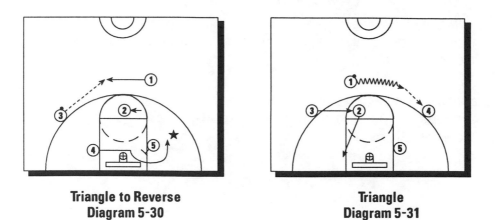

Triangle to Reverse
Diagram 5-30

Triangle
Diagram 5-31

If (3) is not open, the team may run either the basic pattern (see Diagram 5-32) or the jump-shot variation (see Diagram 5-33).

This play involves some teaching and practice time because the players, who are use to being specialists, must learn new assignments.

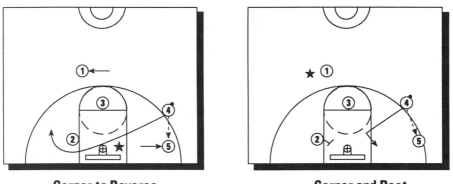

Corner to Reverse
Diagram 5-32

Corner and Post
Diagram 5-33

Pinch-Post Play from the Jump-Shot Variation
Player (1) passes to (3) and cuts away and (2) cuts to the middle. Nothing develops so (4) cuts to the ballside corner or short corner. See Diagram 5-34.

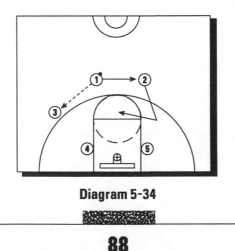

Diagram 5-34

Player (3) passes to (4) in the corner and posts up. See Diagram 5-35. This time, however, (4), after passing to (2) stepping out to the perimeter, screens for (3). See Diagram 5-36.

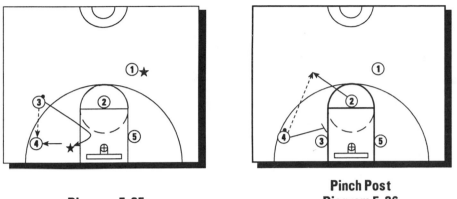

Diagram 5-35

Pinch Post
Diagram 5-36

This screen gives (3) another option. If (2) passes the ball to (1), (3) loops around (5) for a jump shot. See Diagram 5-37.

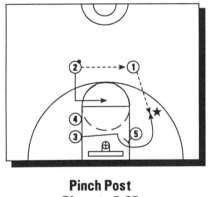

Pinch Post
Diagram 5-37

However, if (2) fakes the ball to (1), (3) may double back and use (4)'s pinch screen to cut to the ballside wing. See Diagram 5-38.

Then if (3) is not open, (2) can pass to (1), and (3) and (4) will change assignments, with (4) looping around (5), and (3) becoming the offside post. See Diagram 5-39.

This option works well because once the defense has seen the jump-shot variation, they tend to anticipate the quick reversal to (3).

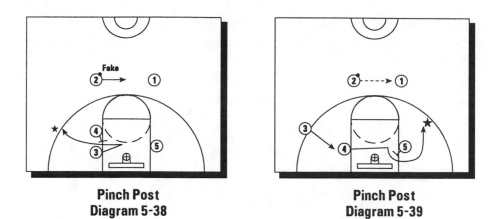

Pinch Post
Diagram 5-38

Pinch Post
Diagram 5-39

Weakside Dribble-Entry Play from the 2-3 Set

Diagram 5-40 shows the weakside guard (2) make a dribble entry to the open forward position on the side. This tells the offside forward (3) to cut to the middle.

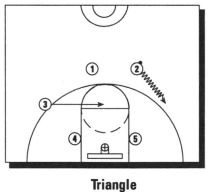

Triangle
Diagram 5-40

If the triangle play is not open, the ballside post (5) may cut to the corner and either the basic pattern (see Diagram 5-41) or the jump-shot option (see Diagram 5-42) may be run.

This dribble-entry play allows the weakside guard to initiate the pattern and presents a new picture to the defense.

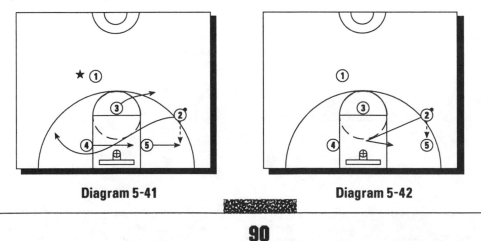

Diagram 5-41

Diagram 5-42

Strongside Dribble-Entry Play from the 2-3 Set

Diagram 5-43 shows strongside guard (1) dribbling at and clearing forward (3) down and around the ballside post (4), and to the high-post area.

From there, either the basic pattern (see Diagram 5-44) or the jump-shot option (see Diagram 5-45) may be run.

This play works best when (1) is of adequate size and inside strength.

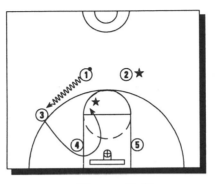

Diagram 5-43

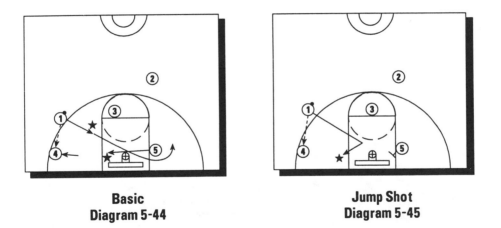

Basic
Diagram 5-44

Jump Shot
Diagram 5-45

Guard Choice Stack Play

This stack play is run from a two-guard, (1) and (2), front, with two post players (4) and (5), and forward (3) stacked under post (4). See Diagram 5-46.

Player (1) passes to (2) and cuts down the lane. Player (1) may cut either of two ways: around the double screen of (4) and (3), or around (5)'s single downscreen. Player (3) will key on (1)'s cut and always go opposite. See Diagram 5-47.

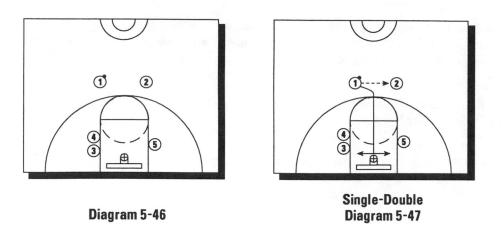

Diagram 5-46

Single-Double
Diagram 5-47

Double-Screen Cut Option

Diagram 5-48 shows (1) cutting around the double screen of (4) and (3), who attempt to trap the zone inside. Player (3) then crosses the lane (following the rule to go opposite (1)) and cuts around a downscreen by (5), who attempts to trap the zone inside.

Player (2) may then pass to either wing (as to (1) in Diagram 5-49). This tells the offside wing (3) to cut to the middle. From there, the basic pattern or the jump-shot variation may be run from the 1-2-2 set.

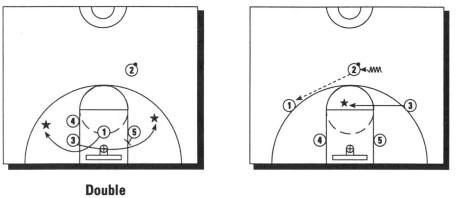

Double
Diagram 5-48

Diagram 5-49

Single-Screen Cut Option

Diagram 5-50 shows (1) passing to (2), cutting down the lane, and around the single screen set by (5), who attempts to trap the zone inside. Player (3) again goes opposite (1) by popping to the wing on the side; (4) attempts to trap the zone inside by downscreening for (3).

Player (2) may then pass to either wing (as to (1) in Diagram 5-51). This tells the offside wing (3) to cut to the middle for a triangle play.

The team is then in position to run the basic pattern or the strong jump-shooter pattern from the 1-2-2 set.

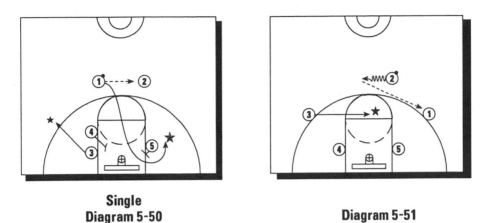

Single
Diagram 5-50

Diagram 5-51

This inside-oriented offense thoroughly tests the zone's most vulnerable areas, which are the middle and corner. It also uses other zone offensive fundamentals, such as overloading, overshifting, changing the perimeter, splitting the zone, and utilizing the offensive players' strengths. For the best results, pick the set that fits your players and start with the basic pattern. Add the strong jump-shot option early in the season and use the auxiliary plays only if necessary.

Player Movement Versus Zones

This chapter contrasts two diverse methods of executing zone offense. The chapter starts with another motion-oriented zone offense and finishes with a look at a basic static zone offense, and two novel ideas in minimum motion zone offense. You, the coach, can choose the approach that best fits your offensive philosophy and the personnel you have available.

Movement Versus Zones

Many coaches insist that player movement is necessary in zone offenses. Some of the reasons they offer are:

1. Player movement presents a varying perimeter to the zone defenders.

2. Cuts through the zone cause the defense to contract and make perimeter coverage more difficult.

3. Movement permits a team to vary its attack and test all the vital areas of the zone defense.

4. Defensive players cannot easily anticipate the next offensive sequence in their area. This limits the size of the sag they can make when the ball goes away from them. This, in turn, gives the offensive team more room to penetrate the middle of the zone.

5. Moving offensive players are more alert. Offensive maneuvers work better on the move, and you are also more apt to charge the offensive boards.

6. A coach can design specific patterns to work against a given team.

7. The weaker player, who cannot beat the defender one-on-one, may get open via the pattern.

Following is an offense based on player movement.

The Motion-Oriented Zone Offense

This offense tests the zone in many ways. The motion offers a constantly varying perimeter, the plays are a series of attempts to overload and overshift the defense, and there is the constant threat of the big player in the middle if the defense becomes too perimeter conscious.

Personnel Alignment

The offense is designed for a team with four agile perimeter shooters and one strong inside player. It is initiated from a (1) and (2) two-guard front with two forwards, (3) and (4), who start at the free throw line extended; and the big post (5), who, in most cases, stays between the ball and the basket. See Diagram 6-1.

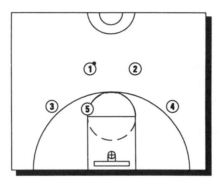

Diagram 6-1

The Basic Pattern

The basic pattern begins as a guard ((1) in Diagram 6-2) passes to (3), the forward on (1)'s side. This tells the offside guard (2) to cut through to the ballside corner. Post (5) then swings to the ballside. The offside forward (4) drops to a position between the ball and the offside corner to assume rebounding position.

This overload is then utilized as the ball is passed around the triangles formed by (1), (3), (5), and (2). See Diagram 6-3.

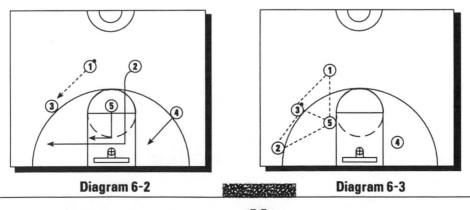

Diagram 6-2   Diagram 6-3

The onside wing (3) is the player who may choose to change the side of the overload. (3) does this in either of two ways. Player (3) may pass to the corner (to (2)) and cut through to the offside, or pass to the point (to (1)) and cut through to the offside.

Pass to the Corner

When (3) passes to (2) in the corner and cuts through, the other perimeter players rotate to fill the open areas. Player (1) moves to replace (3), and (4) takes the point. See Diagram 6-4. The ball is then reversed to (3) at the offside wing. See Diagram 6-5.

This reversal tells (2), who is the baseline roamer, and post (5) to swing to the ballside. See Diagram 6-6.

From there the passing triangle overload is utilized until (3) decides to change it again.

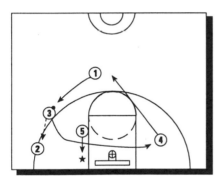

Overload
Diagram 6-4

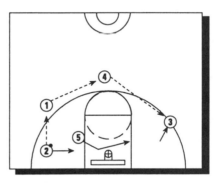

Reverse
Diagram 6-5

Overload
Diagram 6-6

Pass to the Point

This time (3), who is again the ballside wing player, decides to change the overload by passing to (4) at the point. After the pass, (3) cuts through to the offside corner and (2) replaces (3) at the wing. See Diagram 6-7. Player (3) has now become the baseline roamer.

The ball is then passed to (1) on the offside. Post (5) swings to that side as (2) assumes the offside wing position. See Diagram 6-8. The new overload triangles are then utilized until (1), who has become the ballside wing, decides to change the overload.

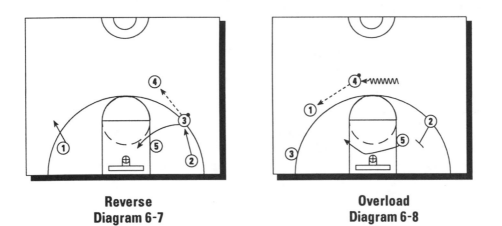

Reverse
Diagram 6-7

Overload
Diagram 6-8

This constant flow of cuts through the zone results in overload triangles, thoroughly tests the defense, and provides high-percentage shots.

Auxiliary Plays

At this point, the key components of the offense have been presented. The auxiliary plays are used when and if a change is needed to meet specific situations or to add depth to the offense as the season progresses.

Last-Shot Double-Screen Play

As the team seeks a last shot, (1) passes to the forward (3) and calls out "double." Player (2), the offside guard, cuts toward the ballside corner, but stops in the low-post area below post (5). See Diagram 6-9.

Player (3) returns the ball to (1) and cuts over the double screen of (5) and (2). Player (1) dribbles toward the offside guard position as (4) moves to the side of the double screen. See Diagrams 6-10 and 6-11.

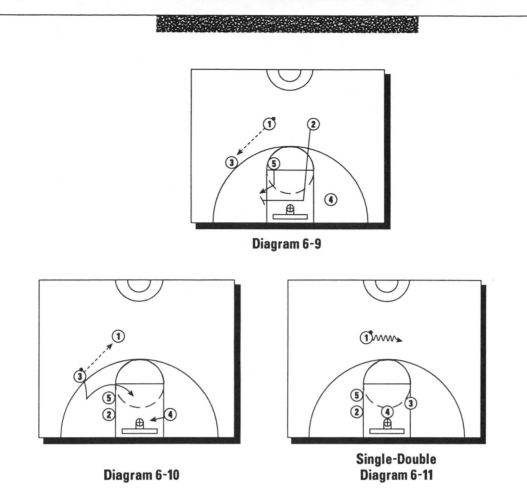

Diagram 6-9

Diagram 6-10

**Single-Double
Diagram 6-11**

Player (1) then stops, fakes to (5), and attempts to pass to (4), looping around the double screen; (2) and (5) try to trap the zone inside and prevent the defenders from getting to (4). See Diagram 6-12.

If (4) receives the ball and cannot shoot, (2) moves to the ballside corner and the basic overload motion is resumed. See Diagram 6-13.

Player (4) is now the ballside wing and can change the overload when desired.

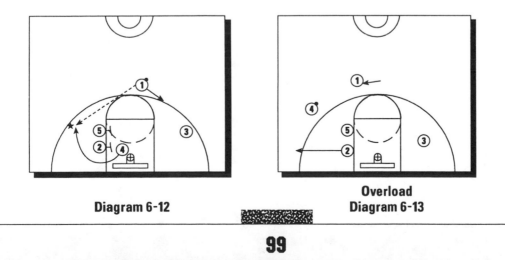

Diagram 6-12

**Overload
Diagram 6-13**

Adjusting Zone Play

When playing against adjusting zones, which attempt to match the offensive perimeter, the following option may be added. The guard making the initial pass ((1) to (3) in Diagram 6-14) cuts through to the offside wing and the offside wing (4) cuts to the ballside corner.

This still permits the same pass-to-corner and pass-to-point options. It has a further advantage if (3) will first use a pass-to-the-point option and cut to (1)'s corner. See Diagram 6-15.

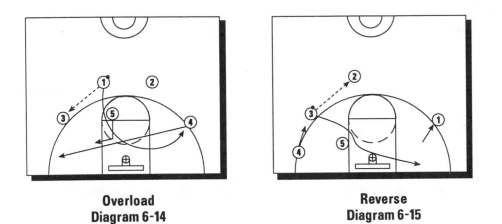

Overload
Diagram 6-14

Reverse
Diagram 6-15

The ball is then reversed to (1)'s side who may: (A) pass the ball around the perimeter seeking an outside shot, (B) use the pass-to-point option, (C) use the pass-to-corner option, or (D) when playing against matching zones, dribble out front and return the offense to a two-player front. See Diagrams 6-16 and 6-17.

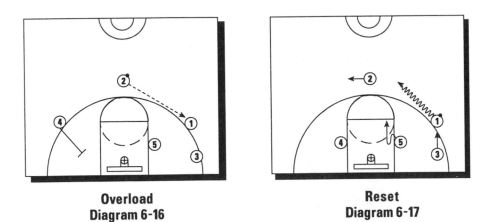

Overload
Diagram 6-16

Reset
Diagram 6-17

Since this adjusting zone play returns the offense to a two-player (even) front, it forces the zone to adjust in order to match the offensive perimeter. This may lead to defensive errors. Once the defense has adjusted, the offense may again send a guard through and return to an odd front. See Diagrams 6-18 and 6-19.

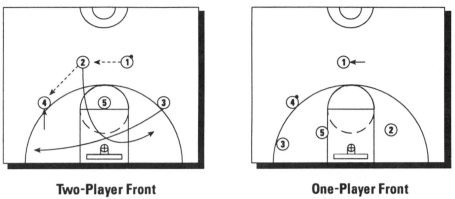

Two-Player Front
Diagram 6-18

One-Player Front
Diagram 6-19

Split-Lob Play from the Basic Pattern

Once (2) has cut through to the ballside corner and an overload has been formed, the split-lob play may be run. In Diagram 6-20, (3), the ballside forward, has the ball and keys the play by making an emphatic fake to (2) in the corner. This does two things. It pulls a defender to (2). It also tells (4) to break to the high post area.

Player (3) passes to (4), and (5) steps up to screen for (3); (3) then cuts off (5) for the lob pass. If (3) can cut inside X3, the defender on (2), the lob pass has a chance to work because the middle defender of the zone will be covering (5). Player (2) uses (3)'s cut to form a splitting action as (2) cuts to the wing area. See Diagram 6-21.

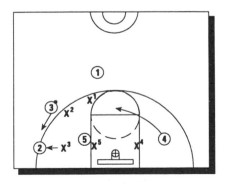

Diagram 6-20

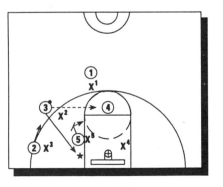

Split Lob
Diagram 6-21

If (3) is not open, (4) should look for (2), cutting to the wing because once the pass is made to (4), the zone may attempt to jam the middle and leave the perimeter wide open. See Diagrams 6-22 and 6-23.

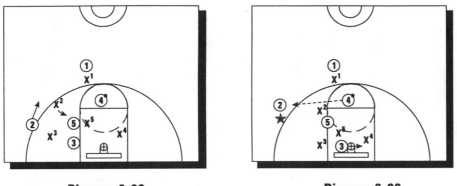

| Diagram 6-22 | Diagram 6-23 |

If nothing develops, (4) may pass the ball out to (1), who resets the offense by dribbling away from (2) to pull him or her out front. See Diagrams 6-24 and 6-25.

Motion can be functional in a zone offense, but if it is done incorrectly or to excess, it can lessen the team's chance to obtain a well-balanced, squared up, high-percentage shot in a context that provides a rebound plan. To avoid this problem, much teaching must be done in regard to being aware of when shots should occur and receiving the ball in an all-purpose position that facilitates shooting, passing, dribbling, or pivoting. The guideline to follow is "move with a purpose."

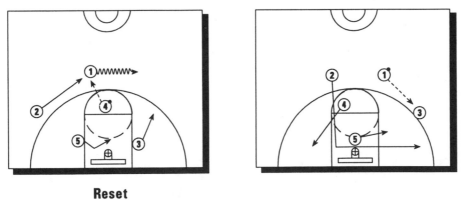

Reset
Diagram 6-24

Diagram 6-25

Minimum Motion Zone Offenses

Many coaches prefer static offenses that require a minimum of movement. Some of the reasons they offer are:

1. Static offenses allow the players to become specialists. For example, big players develop inside power moves and learn they are the primary rebounders.

2. Perimeter players can become very adept shooters from a particular area of the floor by devoting much practice time to it.

3. The offense can take advantage of personnel match-ups. For example, a coach can place the best shooter in the area covered by their worst defender, or put the tall players on the side where their small players are located and then plan many shots from the opposite side to take advantage of this rebounding edge.

4. Once those primarily responsible for rebounding have been determined, it is easy to make assignments to determine defensive balance.

5. When a player is not required to be overly pattern conscious, he or she is free to think about basic things, such as getting into position to shoot or to rebound.

6. Not moving facilitates the establishments of a planned functional passing tempo without the constraints of timing a pattern.

7. More big players may be used, who may lack the skill and agility to execute fundamentals while in motion.

Coaches preferring this minimum motion approach desire a static plan that may be used against odd- or even-front zones, that takes advantage of the attributes of their personnel, and that provides for defensive balance and offensive rebounding. The following plans meet most of those requirements. The first offense is the basic static zone offense and the other two are novel approaches to minimum motion zone offense. They are for those coaches who have looked at the offenses in the previous chapter and are still wary of too much movement versus zone defenses.

Static Zone Offense

The only movement in this offense is that which allows it to adjust its perimeter in order to split odd and even zones. It starts in a 2-3 box and adjusts, if necessary.

2-3 Box Alignment

The 2-3 box formation is used against odd-front zones (1-3-1, 1-2-2, 3-2). The best personnel for this set would include two guards (1) and (2) of average size with the ability to hit the 12- to 15-foot jump shot, and two fairly tall forwards (3) and (4) who can shoot from the free throw line extended and rebound from the offside. The post (5) must be big, strong on the boards, and able to score with his or her back to the basket. Player (5) is the team's primary rebounder. See Diagram 6-26.

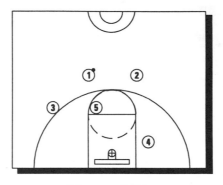

Diagram 6-26

Rules of Position Adjustment

We speak in terms of position adjustments instead of motion because this offense has very little movement. The players must make the following position adjustments. Post (5) should stay between the ball and the basket at all times on the post line. The ballside forward should be as high as the free throw line extended, and the offside forward should stay between the ball and the offside corner. The offside guard plays as high as the ball and the ballside guard remains out front to provide a passing outlet, and in position to be the first player back on defense. Diagrams 6-27 through 6-30 show these rules in action as the ball is moved around the perimeter.

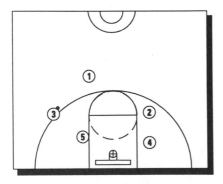

Diagram 6-27

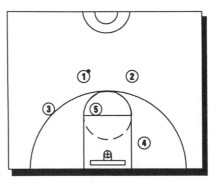

Diagram 6-28

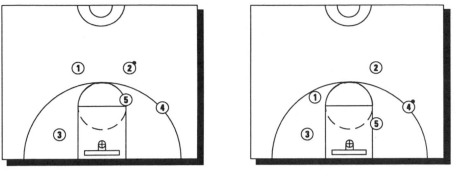

Diagram 6-29   **Diagram 6-30**

When the ball is passed into the high post, (5) should catch and face, shoot, or look for the offside forward inside the zone. See Diagram 6-31.

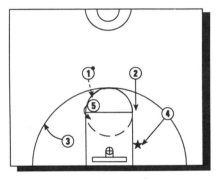

Diagram 6-31

When the ball is passed to (5) in the low post, he or she should shoot unless the zone collapses. This would tell (5) to pass the ball back out to a perimeter player. Player (5) must be taught that pivot shots from the low-post area are high-percentage shots, seem to draw a lot of fouls, and lead to many second (follow-up) shots.

2-3 Box to the 1-3-1 Set

If the zone matches the 2-3 offensive perimeter, the offside guard should cut through and become the baseline roamer. Diagram 6-32 shows (1) passing to forward (3), and (2) cutting to the ballside corner. This move should permit the offense to split the 2-3 zone. Once this has been done, the rules for the offensive players are very much the same. Post (5) still stays between the ball and the basket, forwards (3) and (4) play up on the ballside and down on the offside. Point (1) always plays at an extension of the lane line on the ballside, and the baseline roamer (2) plays in the ballside corner or short corner. Diagrams 6-33 through 6-36 show these rules in action.

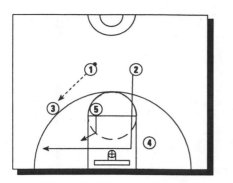

Diagram 6-32

One-Player Front
Diagram 6-33

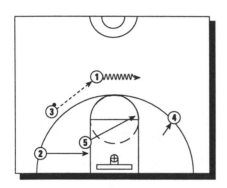

Diagram 6-34

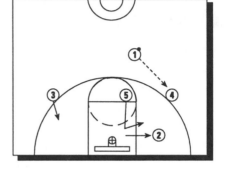

Diagram 6-35

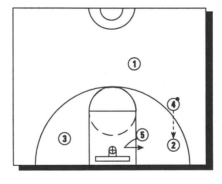

Diagram 6-36

Returning to the 2-3 Box from the 1-3-1 Set

When the team is in a 1-3-1 set and desires to return to a 2-3 set, guard (1) makes a hand signal and dribbles away from the baseline roamer (2). This tells the forward on that side ((4) in Diagram 6-37) to screen down for (2). Player (2) moves first to the wing and may get a pass from (1) for a jump shot; (1) fakes to (3) and then looks for (2) at the wing.

If (2) is not open for a shot, he or she looks to the offside guard position and the team is back in the 2-3 box formation. See Diagram 6-38.

These simple rules permit a team to start in a box formation against odd front zones. If the zone adjusts to a two-player front, the guard (2) goes through and changes the offense to a 1-3-1 set that splits it. If the zone makes a second adjustment, the point (1) dribbles away from the baseline roamer. This brings (2) back out front and again splits the offense. Once the defense is split, the players must move the ball and take the open shot.

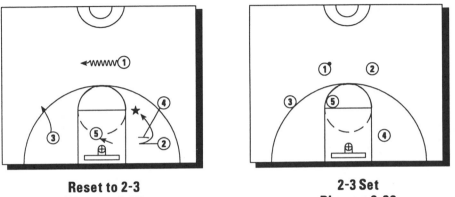

Reset to 2-3
Diagram 6-37

2-3 Set
Diagram 6-38

Offside Forward Key Zone offense

Another plan that requires a minimum of motion but is adjustable to meet various zones is "the offside forward key zone offense."

Personnel Alignment
This offense begins in a 2-3 set with the guard (1) and (2) as wide as the lane, forwards (3) and (4) on their respective sides, and at the free throw line extended, and post (5) in the high post and between the ball and the basket. See Diagram 6-39.

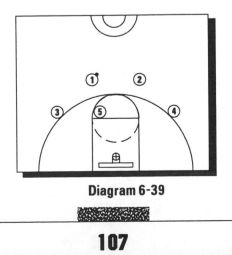

Diagram 6-39

The Basic Plan

When an adjustment from the 2-3 set is desired, guard (1) will initiate it by passing to the forward (3) and cutting down the lane and to the offside. See Diagram 6-40.

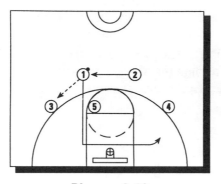

Diagram 6-40

Although (1)'s cut initiates the adjustments, the offside forward (4) actually determines what they will be. After (1) cuts through, (4) may: (A) move out front and maintain the basic 2-3 formation, (B) take the high post and convert the offense to a 1-3-1 tandem post with (4) in the high post and big player (5) in the low post, or (C) screen down for (1) as the player moves across the lane, and then become the baseline roamer of a 1-3-1 offense. Examples of (4)'s options are shown as follows.

(A) Maintain the 2-3 Formation

Diagram 6-41 shows (4) cutting out front. This move keeps the offense in a 2-3 set and is effective versus odd-front zones (1-2-2, 1-3-1, and 3-2). Note that (5) stayed between the ball and the basket and (1) between the ball and the offside corner.

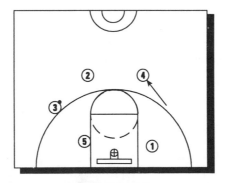

Maintain 2-3
Diagram 6-41

(B) Form the Tandem Post

Diagram 6-42 shows (4) cutting to the high-post area. This converts the offense to a 1-3-1 tandem post set and makes it effective against even-front zones.

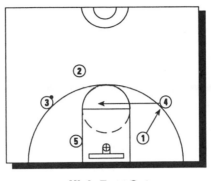

High-Post Cut
Diagram 6-42

If (3) can pass to (4), (5) may be open inside the zone or (1) may have a jump shot at the offside wing. If nothing develops, the ball is moved around the perimeter with (1), (2), and (3) the outside players, (4) as the ballside high post, and (5) as the offside low post. See Diagrams 6-43 and 6-44.

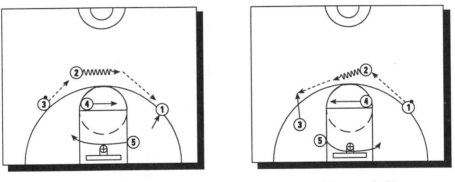

Diagram 6-43   **Diagram 6-44**

(C) Screen Down for (1) and Become the 1-3-1 Baseline Roamer

Diagram 6-45 shows (4) screening down for (1) after (1)'s cut through. Player (3) reverses the ball to (1) coming off (4)'s downscreen for a possible jump shot. See Diagram 6-46.

The offense is now aligned in a 1-3-1 set with a baseline roamer (4). This permits the team to overload the zone.

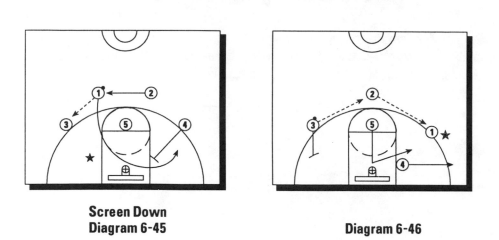

**Screen Down
Diagram 6-45**

Diagram 6-46

Thus (4) may call the play and decide the formation. Player (4)'s cut out front keeps the team in a 2-3 set. His or her cut to the high-post keys a 1-3-1 tandem post. If (4) decides to screen down for (1), it calls a 1-3-1 formation with a baseline roamer and permits the team to overload the zone. Once an alignment has been designated, the team stays in it until a shot has been taken.

Dribble-Entry Option

This same principle may be used with a dribble entry. Diagram 6-47 shows (1) dribbling at and clearing (3) to the offside. Player (4) may then:

(A) Move out front to maintain the 2-3 alignment.

(B) Take the high post to form a 1-3-1 tandem post ((4) and (5)). See Diagrams 6-48 and 6-49.

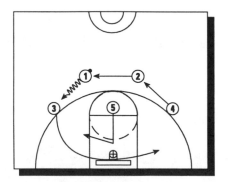

**Dribble Entry
Diagram 6-47**

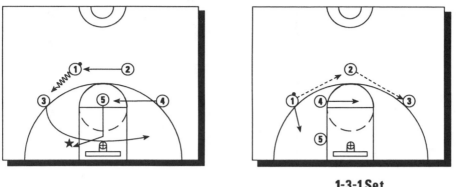

Diagram 6-48

1-3-1 Set
Diagram 6-49

(C) Screen down for (3) and convert the offense to a 1-3-1 with a baseline roamer and create overloading potential. See Diagrams 6-50 and 6-51.

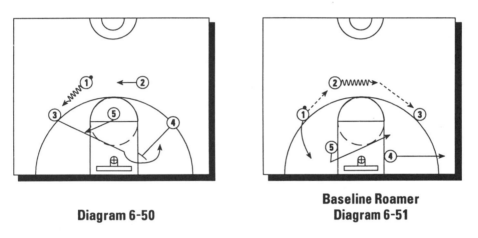

Diagram 6-50

Baseline Roamer
Diagram 6-51

Monster Zone Offense

A plan that is very similar to "the forward key zone offense" is "the monster zone offense."

Personnel Alignment
This offense is run from a 1-4 set that includes point (1), two wings (2) and (3) at the free throw line extended, and two high posts (4) and (5). See diagram 6-52.

The ball is moved around the 1-4 set perimeter until point (1) decides to key a change of formation by raising the off arm and dribbling to one side. (Player (5) is the smaller of the two posts so it is preferable for (1) to dribble away from (5).) This makes (5) the offside post (the monster) who will determine the new formation. See Diagram 6-53.

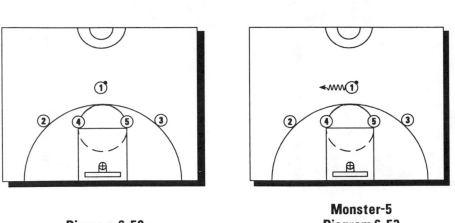

Diagram 6-52

Monster-5
Diagram 6-53

Player (5) may now:

(A) Move out front to the off-guard area. This converts the offense to a 2-3 set. See Diagram 6-54.

(B) Move to the baseline and become the baseline roamer of a 1-3-1 set. See Diagram 6-55.

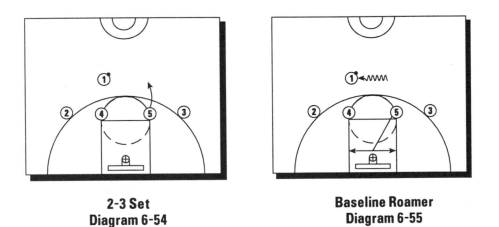

2-3 Set
Diagram 6-54

Baseline Roamer
Diagram 6-55

(C) Drop low and become the low post of a 1-3-1 tandem post set. See Diagrams 6-56 and 6-57.

(D) Stay put and keep the team in the 1-4 set. See Diagram 6-58.

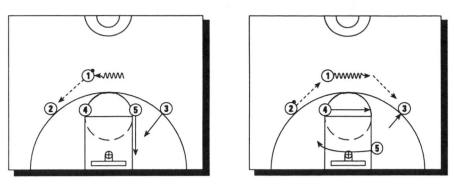

1-3-1 Set
Diagram 6-56

Diagram 6-57

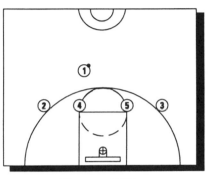

Diagram 6-58

This versatility of the monster zone offense permits four players to do the same job regardless of formation. All adjustments are made by the monster (5) and initiated by (1)'s dribble to the side and a hand signal.

These three offenses require a minimum of cutting, but still allow for changes in the offensive set. They are designed for the coach who feels that a great deal of motion is ineffective against zones.

It must be stressed that the decision you, the coach, make in regard to the amount of motion in your offense, must be dictated by your offensive philosophy and the type of players who will make up your team.

CHAPTER 7

Practicing Winning Zone Offense

This chapter will first deal with basketball practice in general and then move to specific methods that may be used to improve your offensive zone game. It includes such topics as: motivational tips, practice mechanics, preseason practice of zone offense, the zone scouting report, and in-season specific game zone offensive practice.

General Practice methods

The results of your practice planning are not always determined by your knowledge of X's and O's. At least equally important is your ability to work with people. You must be able to motivate them in a positive direction and design the mechanical aspects of your practice sessions to create a viable teaching-learning environment. Following are ten motivational tips that will serve to help you get a better effort from your players and associates, and ten suggestions on how to improve the mechanical aspects of your practice sessions.

Motivational Tips
To motivate is to cause someone to move. The ability to accomplish this feat in a positive direction is a key secret to coaching success. These ten tips will help you in that regard.

1. In order to motivate others, you must maintain a personal desire to do your best. "You can't be a beacon if your light don't shine." Teach your players to be on time, be open (to learning) and be their best.

2. The learning situation you create in practice should be planned to encourage each player to become one's best self.

3. Coaches must come to realize that people react more favorably to praise than to criticism. "Try to catch them in the act of doing something right."

4. End practice on a high note. Send each player home feeling "this is fun, and I am really good at it."

5. When problems occur, attack the problem and not the individual(s) involved.

6. Teach players that failure is an opportunity for creativity and should be used as a guidepost for the future.

7. If you want someone to be something, tell them that is what they are. The words you transmit to their minds will create pictures and thoughts that will add to, or detract from, their ability to perform.

8. Don't use long practices or tough conditioning drills as punishment. Practices and drills should be viewed by the players as positive steps to success.

9. Use the theory of "discipline and freedom." The disciplines of an activity are the nuts-and-bolts fundamentals of a skill or team technique. The freedoms are related drills, games, etc. that are fun, and may be used as a respite from the drudgery of too much concentrated effort. A good teacher or coach stresses the disciplines until it is sensed that interest, concentration, and/or intensity are on the wane. At that point, the coach inserts freedoms to recreate the learning situation. One must be aware that highly motivated individuals can hone in on the disciplines longer than those who lack motivation.

10. Once your players have demonstrated self-motivation, their awareness and ability to learn increase. If you can capture this moment and present them with meaningful information and/or activities, growth and improvement will follow. Become aware of these teachable moments.

Practice Mechanics

The positive motivational ideas should be used within the context of a mechanically sound practice plan. Here are some ideas to consider in regard to proper practice procedures.

1. Have a plan—season, weekly, daily. Keep a daily practice plan and a weekly practice composite. Otherwise, you may spend too much time on one phase of the game while neglecting another.

2. Write down specific goals for each practice segment and emphasize each of them. Consider a practice theme for the day (e.g., Be quick but don't hurry.)

3. Give your helpers specific duties that afford them a level of prestige. Write out a job description for each. Then take the time to sit down and discuss the assignments with each of them individually. This includes coaching assistants and student assistants.

4. Thoughtful repetition is the key to skill development. Seek out drills that provide repetitive opportunities to properly execute the skill. Prefer drills that involve large numbers of teaching stations, balls, and above all, players. Players learn by doing; keep everyone involved. Drills should directly relate to your system and game play.

5. Each practice should be designed to provide sequential, meaningful learning. One way to do this is to start practice by discussing what was learned yesterday, then tell players what will be accomplished today, next teach today's new materials, follow that by reviewing what was covered today, and at the close of practice tell them what we will attempt to accomplish tomorrow.

6. Use many short practice segments. This is in opposition to covering one phase of the game and using one long practice segment. It is also wise to present new material early in the session.

7. Create a winning practice atmosphere. When the time for practice arrives: the training has been completed, the necessary equipment is on the court and in good working condition, the floor has been swept, the practice uniforms are neat and clean, all the personnel (coaches and players) are on the court, the players have warmed up and completed any prepractice requirements, and today's practice plan has been given to, and discussed with, the assistant coach(es).

8. Plan situation practice segments that utilize the clock, involve a specific rule, or require a definition of specific terminology.

9. Blow a sharp whistle in practice. It should signify that we are ready to proceed to the next phase of our plan without delay. This whistle can be used to remind/teach players of fundamentals. This can be done by having them assume a basketball-ready or all-purpose position when the whistle is sounded and until you give them instructions.

10. Coaches dress out for every practice. They are the first to arrive and the last to leave. Use pre- and post-practice time to meet/work with individuals.

Practicing Zone Offense

This section will include practicing zone offense in the preseason and preparing for a specific team during the season.

Preseason Zone Offense Practice

Preseason practice involves much teaching and constant repetition of fundamentals. It is preferable to do these things primarily by way of breakdown drills.

For purposes of explanation, we will use the inside-oriented offense of chapter five. First we will review the offense. It consists of three plays which are: the triangle play (see Diagram 7-1), the corner play (see Diagram 7-2), and the reverse and reset play (see Diagram 7-3).

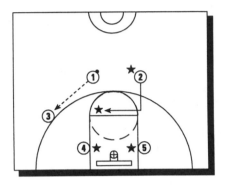

Diagram 7-1

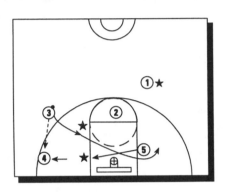

Diagram 7-2

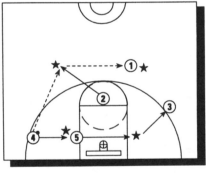

Diagram 7-3

The Walk-Through to Skeleton Offense

The offense is introduce by having five players walk through it as the three parts are explained. At this time, the coach will emphasize the name of each play, the proper spacing and timing, the shot options, the rebound triangle, and defensive balance. The purpose of this phase is to give all players the overall view of the offense, i.e., the big picture. The walk-through progressively proceeds to full speed, whole team execution of the offense as a "skeleton" drill with no defenders. This develops team timing, coordination, rebounding assignments and transition practice.

Breakdown Drills—Skeleton Offense
The next step is to break the offense down into the three drills that provide opportunities for thoughtful repetition. These drills should include the entire squad. While they are being run, the coach must insist on proper execution of the fundamentals. Drills should be directly related to the offense.

Drill #1—The Triangle and Off-Guard Drill
No defense is used for this drill. The guards alternate at the (1) and (2) positions. The small forwards work at the (3) and (4) positions and the large forwards and centers alternate at the (4) and (5) positions. Guards (1) and (2) are at least a step above the head of the key and as wide as the lane. Forward (3) should receive the initial pass from (1) at the free throw line extended and wide. This spacing must be stressed because many players tend to flatten out the offense and this makes it much easier for the opposition. After (1)'s pass to (3), (1) cuts to the offside guard position as (2) moves down and then to the middle of the free throw line area. Player (2) is taught to find a hole in the middle of the zone and be prepared to catch the ball in traffic. This hole may occur above or below the free throw line. At the same time, the ballside post (4) is posting up and (5), the offside post, is establishing rebound position. (See Diagram 7-4.)

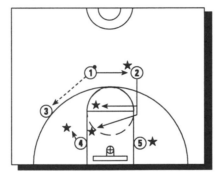

Triangle
Diagram 7-4

From that point, the following options are available.

(A) When (3) shoots: Players (2), (4), and (5) charge the boards from the rebound triangle and (1) stays back for defensive balance; (3) may also attempt to rebound. See Diagram 7-5.

(B) When (3) passes to the ballside post (4): Player (4) usually has room for a one-on-one play in a game situation. After the shot, the rebound triangle plus (3) go to the offensive board and (1) stays back as a safety. See Diagram 7-6.

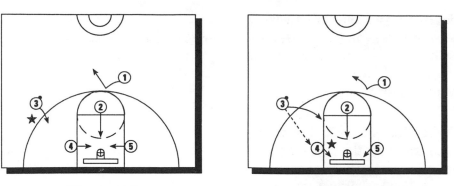

Diagram 7-5   **Diagram 7-6**

(C) When (3) passes crosscourt to (1): Player (1) is instructed to catch the ball in an all-purpose position. This allows him or her to jump shoot, make a dribble penetration if the defense overruns, or pass. Again after the shot, the rebound triangle goes to the boards and (1) stays back; (3) may also become a rebounder. See Diagram 7-7.

(D) When (3) passes to (2) in the high post area: Player (2) may shoot or pass inside to (4) or (5). To facilitate this, (2) is taught to catch the ball in an all-purpose position and then square up to the basket (catch and face). Players (4) and (5) are told to establish position as (2) receives the pass. They do this by spreading out, posting up, and giving (2) a passing target. When the pass is made inside, (4) and (5) expect to shoot a power jump shot off the board or, if possible, to dunk the ball. In a game situation and when closely guarded, they fake once and then power up. See Diagram 7-8.

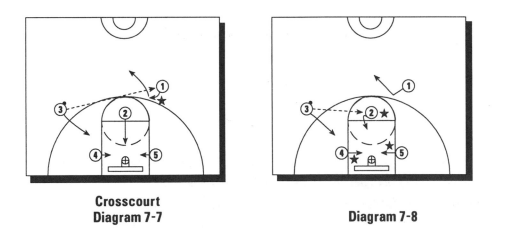

Crosscourt
Diagram 7-7   **Diagram 7-8**

After (3) has made a pass and a shot option has been executed, the five players on the court move off and a new group moves on. The (3) players are instructed not to run the same scoring option twice in a row.

Drill #2—The Corner Drill

No defense is used for this drill. It begins with a triangle play. See Diagram 7-9. Ballside post (4) then keys a corner play by cutting to the ballside corner or short corner. See Diagram 7-10.

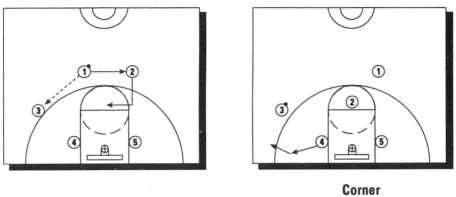

Diagram 7-9

Corner
Diagram 7-10

Player (3) passes to (4) and cuts through, looking for a return pass. This is a difficult pass but the threat of it must be made apparent to the defense. The following options prevail.

(A) If the return pass to (3) is made, (3) must be careful not to be out of control and commit a charging foul. The player is taught to catch the ball while executing a jump stop. Then if open, he or she can move to the basket. Player (4) should aim the pass at (3)'s numbers and not lead him or her to a charging foul. See Diagram 7-11.

(B) If the return pass is not made from (4) to (3), (3) continues across the lane and (5) uses (3) as a natural screen as (5) cuts to the ballside. Player (5) is taught to find the hole in the middle of the zone. It may be found anywhere from the low-post area to the free throw line. This pass from (4) to (5) is a desired option; (4) should take time and make a two-hand overhead pass. See Diagram 7-12.

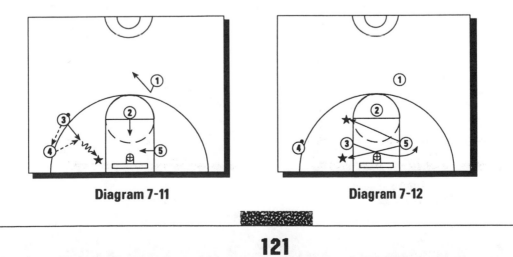

Diagram 7-11

Diagram 7-12

(C)   If the defense is late getting to (4) or falls off, (4) may shoot. See Diagram 7-13.

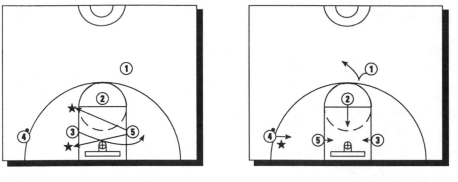

Diagram 7-12   **Diagram 7-13**

On all three of these options, the importance of the rebounding triangle and (1)'s maintenance of defensive balance must be stressed.

Once a shot is taken, five new players take the court to run skeleton offense and the former participants change lines.

Drill #3—The Reverse and Reset Drill

No defense is used for this drill. The pattern is run through the triangle and corner phases and then (2), the guard who cut to the high-post area, must recognize that it is time to cancel the corner play. The player does this by cutting to the ballside. Player (2) receives a pass from (4) and catches it with a jump stop, followed by a pivot to square up to the basket. If (2) does not have a shot, he or she passes to (1). During this time (4) and (5) have drifted back to their original positions. See Diagram 7-14. Player (1) then passes to (3) and restarts the pattern. The coach emphasizes to the perimeter players that they look for their shots as the ball is reversed and that there is a possibility that (4) or (5) may be open inside the zone during this time. See Diagram 7-15.

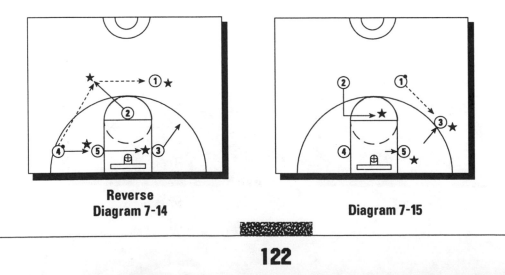

Reverse
Diagram 7-14   **Diagram 7-15**

Repeat Drill #1, #2, and #3 Twice Around—Skeleton Offense

These same three drills are run in sequence, but this time the entire offense is run once around and the scoring options will occur on the second side. Care is again taken to prevent sloppiness in terms of spacing, timing, and the individual fundamentals (passing, catching, stopping, etc.); the importance of maintaining the rebound triangle and defensive balance are stressed.

Scrimmage

Once it has been determine that the team has learned the pattern, scrimmage is the next logical step. However, we feel that scrimmage must be approached in a cautious fashion. Otherwise, the pattern is forgotten and the play becomes ragged. Because of this, the following steps to full-court scrimmage should be utilized.

Step One—Half-Court Scrimmage (Half to Full)

A defense is added and the offense is instructed to run the pattern until a good shot develops. Team "A" is given the ball for five plays and then takes the defense as Team "B" runs the offense for five plays. No freelancing is permitted and all first shots must be taken from the desired shot options. The defending team is allowed to make a quick transition to early offense.

Step Two—Full-Court Scrimmage with No Fast Break

Basketball is a full-court game and too much half-court practice can hurt a team. A different perspective is attained when you take the ball out, bring it upcourt, and then run the pattern. At this point, no fast breaks are allowed and the shots are taken from the desired shot option locations. The defending team can be allowed an early offense transition.

Step Three—Controlled Scrimmage with Limited Fast Breaks

The type of controlled scrimmage preferred is one in which the team that scores gets the ball back at midcourt. This allows for a limited number of fast breaks, but also assures that the pattern will be run.

Step Four—Full Scrimmage

This is the most difficult step of teaching zone offense. You want them to take the fast break when it is there, but to set up and run the pattern when it is not. This usually involves finding a guard willing and able to act as the team's quarterback and to eliminate "in-between plays." An "in-between play" is a shot that is taken (often forced) after the break is over and before the team is in position to run the pattern. These plays often lead to situations where there is no one in position to rebound and no one to provide defensive balance.

The three skeleton drills and four steps to full-court scrimmage should be run in sequence during the early season. After that, the breakdown drills should be utilized when the team is not adequately performing the fundamentals or to teach specific adjustments against a given team.

You should revert back to the four scrimmage steps when your full-court scrimmages become ragged.

Spot Shooting

As has been previously stated, it is smart to determine the shot options of your offense and do a lot of spot shooting from those areas. This offense develops players who are specialists. Therefore, they shoot a great many shots from specific areas. Using the spots shown in Diagram 7-16, player (1) specializes in spots three and five, player (2) shoots from spots three and five, plus the six; and big players (4) and (5) work at the corner spots one and seven, plus playing one-on-one in the post position. Each player is instructed to make a certain number of shots from each of the spots after practice. The player then records the number of attempts it took to make them with the manager.

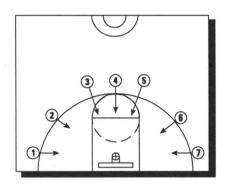

Diagram 7-16

In-Season Game Week Zone Offense Practice

During the week of a game, you may use the breakdown drills to teach the adjustments that are to be made for this particular team.

The Scouting Report and Its Use

The data in the scouting report will be the basis of any alteration in the basic zone offense. Here are some adjustments that may be considered. The questions are from one of our scouting reports on an opponent and are followed by possible strategies we could adopt.

1. What is the shape/sets of their zone?

If it was found that their zone had an even front, we could run the inside-oriented zone offense from an odd front to comply with the even-odd rule. See Diagram 7-17.

Diagram 7-17

2. What is the obvious intent of their zone?

If they were pressuring the perimeter, we would stress getting the ball inside. If they were jamming the lane, we would work extra hard on the perimeter shots or plan to hold the ball and pull them out.

3. When you split their initial alignment, do they match up?

If so, we would plan to send a cutter through after they made their rotation.

4. Do they match up throughout the entire offensive sequence?

If they do, we would plan to constantly vary the offensive perimeter.

5. Which is their weaker defensive side?

We might plan to work the weaker side more often and/or to make personnel adjustments. This might involve such things as placing our best shooter on their weaker defensive side.

6. Which is their strongest rebounding side?

We could plan to work to that side a lot and force the strong rebounders to come out and play defense. At the same time, we could put our strong rebounders on the other side.

7. Do they cover the second side in the same manner that they cover the area of initial penetration?

If the answer is no, we might plan to go second side each time without exception.

8. Do they initially tip or cheat their zone to a particular side?

Many zones tip to the offensive right side because most plays are run on that side. See Diagram 7-18. In that case, we might initiate the offense on the other side.

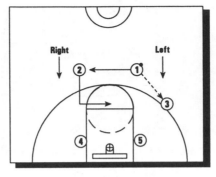

Diagram 7-18

9. Who covers passes to the high post?

For us, this would come into play during the triangle phase of the offense.

If they cover the high post with the offside guard, we would work on the pass from (3) to (1) in the offside guard area. See Diagram 7-19.

If they have an inside defender come up to cover the high post, we would feature the triangle play. See Diagram 7-20.

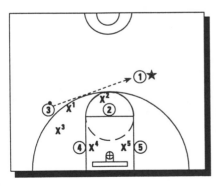

Diagram 7-19

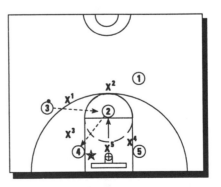

Diagram 7-20

10. How do they react to cutters?

We would work on this during the corner play phase of our offense.

If they ignore cutters, (4) would make the return pass to (3), as (3) cuts through. See Diagram 7-21.

If they go through with the cutters, we would plan for the release player of the corner play (2) to take a jump shot. This might involve (2) moving out early in the cut to the ballside. See Diagram 7-22.

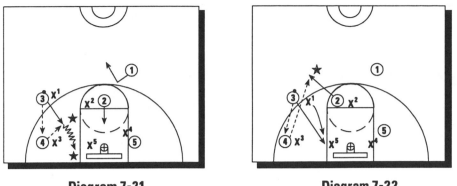

Diagram 7-21   **Diagram 7-22**

11. How do they handle penetration dribbles?

If the defensive inside players are cautious, the dribbler should expect to stop and jump shoot.

If the inside players come up in a reckless fashion, the dribbler may be able to pass to an inside offense player (see (1) in the pass to the offside guard option of the triangle play in Diagram 7-23). There is also a chance that a dribble penetration can be made by the perimeter players during the reverse and reset phase, i.e., penetrate and pitch options should be explored.

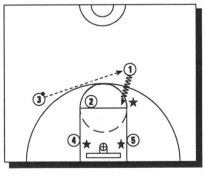

Diagram 7-23

12. How do they handle a rotation dribble?

If the defender guarding the dribbler goes along, we may be able to pass to a release player or loop cutter.

If they switch, we may be able to pass the ball inside.

We would decide if there is any merit in initiating the offense this week via a dribble entry.

13. How do they cover the corner?

Two examples of what could happen during our corner play are:

If the wing defender X1 makes a triangle when the ball is passed to the corner, the release player may be open for a jump shot. See Diagrams 7-24 and 7-25.

 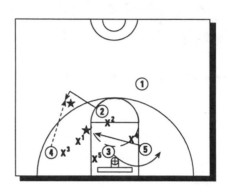

Diagram 7-24   **Diagram 7-25**

If the wing defender X1 makes a move that jams the perimeter passing lanes, we can get the ball inside to (5). See Diagrams 7-26 and 7-27.

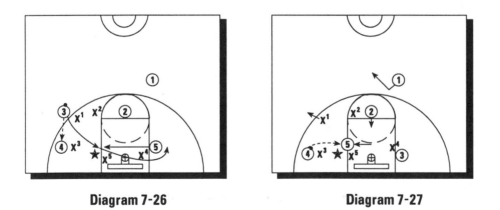

Diagram 7-26   **Diagram 7-27**

14. Do they have an inside player we can overpower?

If so, we would run the corner play in a fashion that would constantly exploit that player. This is an important play to have in your plans because low post, one-on-one plays are high-percentage shots and lead to many free throws and second shots.

15. Do they have a blockout plan?

If they don't, we can point it out in the rebound triangle. If they do, we can show them how to avoid it.

16. Did the opposition do anything that gave the zone problems?

I don't believe in radical changes, but we may be able to find likenesses in our basic plan and exploit them.

17. How do they cover "skip" or crosscourt passes?

If they cover them in a cautious manner and play their zone from the inside out, the receiver will expect to jump shoot.

If they tend to overrun skip pass receivers in poor close-out stances, the offensive player should consider a penetration dribble.

This situation is most apt to occur during the forward (3)-to-guard (1) phase of our triangle play. Although this play is not technically a skip pass, it presents the same type of defensive problem.

18. Do they plug, chest, or make contact with offside cutters?

If they do not, we should plan to run our triangle play quite often as pass to (2).

If they do, the forward (3) should expect to use the other options of the triangle play (ballside post pass or offside guard pass) more often.

19. How do they guard the ballside post player?

If they play behind the post, it should be easy to get the ball inside.

If they front the post, we may resort to lob passes.

If they play three-quarters, the post player will have to create passing angles and seal the defender.

We will work on this during the corner (4)-to-post (5) pass phase of our corner play.

20. What are their basic zone slides?

We will have an assistant coach teach the slides to a scout team early in the week and use them to practice against.

However, before making any changes in our basic plan, we would be sure of the answers to two questions. Will our basic plan suffice? Can we justify the extra practice time these changes will take in terms of the potential benefits?

The importance of motivating players in a positive fashion cannot be overemphasized. This should be done in the context of a well-organized practice plan. In preseason you teach the basic offense in a sequential repetitive manner, while stressing the desired fundamentals. Your approach to scrimmage should be a gradual one that progresses from half-court to full, to full-court with no fast breaks, to full-court controlled scrimmage, to an all-out, but not reckless, full-court game. Once the season starts, the scouting report is the basis of any specific adjustments for a particular team. These adjustments are used only after you are sure the basic plan will not suffice and that the benefits they offer justify the practice time they will require.

THE AUTHORS

As the basketball coach at Eastern Montana College (now Montana State University-Billings) for sixteen seasons, Coach Harkins' teams won 295 games, ten NAIA district titles, and twelve conference championships. He also coached four teams in international competition.

Coach Harkins also served as Professor of Health, Physical Education and Recreation at Eastern Montana College, where he received the college's award for outstanding achievement in scholarship and creativity. In addition, he was awarded Akron University's Distinguished Alumni Award.

Jerry Krause has coached basketball at elementary, secondary, college and Olympic developmental levels for over 34 years. He served for 30 years as research chairman for the National Association of Basketball Coaches. Krause has served as President of the NAIA Basketball Coaches Association and also on the Board of Directors of the NABC. He has served the longest tenure (15 years) of anyone on the NCAA Basketball Rules Committee where he was also chairman. He is most respected for his emphasis (books and videos) on the fundamental skills of basketball. Krause is presently Professor of Sport Philosophy at the United States Military Academy in West Point, New York.

ADDITIONAL BASKETBALL RESOURCES FROM

COACHES CHOICE